FOOTLOOSE IN JERUSALEM

Eight guided walking tours
illustrated with maps
and nineteenth-century engravings
updated edition

BY SARAH FOX KAMINKER

CROWN PUBLISHERS, INC.
NEW YORK

Inquiries should be addressed to Crown Publishers, Inc., One Park Avenue, New York, New York 10016.

Printed in the United States of America

Published simultaneously in Canada by General Publishing Company Limited

Library of Congress Cataloging in Publication Data
Kaminker, Sarah Fox.
Footloose in Jerusalem.
1. Jerusalem—Description—Guide-books.
I. Title.
DS109.K3175 1981   915.694'4045   80-22164
ISBN: 0-517-542943
Originally published by the Center for Jewish Education in the Diaspora of the Hebrew University of Jerusalem
First American edition published 1981 by Crown Publishers, Inc.

10   9   8   7   6   5   4   3   2   1

For the Boys, who preferred to sit this one out
and
For Sheila, a delightful walking companion

CONTENTS

FOOTNOTES
TO FOOTLOOSE

In 1967, on a sunny morning right after the Six-Day War, the concrete wall that had divided Jerusalem in two for 19 years was pulled down. The people of East Jerusalem streamed into West Jerusalem, visiting vaguely remembered and barely recognizable neighborhoods, pointing up at the balconies they had played on as children, marveling at the stoplights, losing their way and finding it again on the new-old street system. On that same morning West Jerusalemites walked over no-man's land and through the gates of the Old City in a joyous journey of discovery and rediscovery. For those who participated in it, that particular early-morning walk will always be cherished as a very special experience.

But for 3,000 years Jerusalem has been a very special experience and the more leisurely, less tumultuous walks of discovery that Jerusalemites take throughout their city as a regular leisure-time activity have a quiet excitement of their own. Visitors and newcomers who want to "go native" are invited to share this experience.

After the Six-Day War, myself a newcomer, I spent each morning strolling through the Old City and its surroundings in my professional capacity as a city planner for the National Parks Authority. Equipped with old maps, colored pencils and a hot bagel which I bought from the open-hearth bakery in Yemin Moshe (it disappeared in the dust of a grand urban renewal project and more's the pity), I set out each morning to explore, to ask questions, and to record. I had a splendid time.

In 1968 and 1969 the streets of Jerusalem were packed with college-aged youngsters, knapsacks on their backs, taking their first searching trips around the world. I was sure that they would leave Jerusalem having learned nothing about it, seeing only the surface and getting bored on tour buses — if they were so lacking in youthful self-respect as to board one. I was sure they were not having a splendid time and — even more — that they were missing the opportunity to participate in the greatest adventure Jerusalem can offer: getting to know it.

I approached Dr. Hanoch Rinot, then director of the Center for Jewish Education of the Hebrew University, with the proposal that we prepare a book of walks for college-aged students. He and his staff members, Barry Chazin, Yigi Brukenstein and Zvi Gastwirth, agreed readily and were most helpful in producing the experimental edition, which contained four walks. By the next year, 1971, four more walks were added and every year thousands of young people and their elders from English-speaking countries were roaming through Jerusalem on the paths outlined in the book.

I tried to persuade complaining property owners along the routes that by opening their gardens to the descending hordes of walkers they were making a contribution to world-wide consciousness about our beloved city — with only moderate success. It is possible that even today you will find a sign on the front of a house or institution that says "This place is closed to walkers using *Footloose in Jerusalem.*"

Every subsequent printing was revised slightly but in the nine years since the first walks were written the face of Jerusalem has changed so substantially that a thorough revamping was required, and the current edition is that revamping.

This book provides no photographs or drawings of contemporary scenes and that is because I feel that everything should be seen first through your own eyes and not as filtered through the sensibilities of someone else. Books on Jerusalem with spectacular illustrations are available in abundance and you should certainly acquire one as the best possible souvenir of your trip to Jerusalem. Engravings from the 1800's have been included in this edition so that you can see some of the changes that have taken place in Jerusalem over the past century and more.

The first five walks in the book will take you on paths outside the walls of the Old City, but each, except for one, ends with a view of the Old City from a different vantage point. Often, the end of one is not far from the beginning of the next and you may continue from one into the other with only a slight break. On the other hand, you may give out before one walk has been completed. In that case, watch out for the midway point provided in almost every walk which will enable you to stop walking at a place convenient to public transportation and to return some other time to complete the walk with renewed strength. By using this device you will find that you are taking 13 walks rather than only eight. Since it is by now clear that older people, indeed very much older people, are using this book as much as or even more than young people, the "midway point" device is my gift to them.

I take this opportunity to thank many colleagues and friends who walked with me and argued with me and responded openly to everything they saw and heard, as one must when walking through Jerusalem. None of them spared me their advice, as is often true with friends and colleagues, and more often than not their comments were incorporated into the text of this book. Among them I would like to thank Shimon Arzi, Gavriel Barkai, Dr. Magen Broshi, Vera Leifman and Golda Werman.

To Joseph Gadish a very special note of gratitude for helping me to be entirely other than "footloose" in all practical matters.

Sarah Kaminker
Jerusalem

AN INTRODUCTION
TO JERUSALEM

A tourist who follows the well-worn sightseeing routes in Jerusalem will see much that is beautiful and more that is significant, but he will rarely reach within the impressive exterior to the complex internal life of the city.

Jerusalem has many facets. It is the Eternal City, with archaeological treasures dating as far back as its first prehistoric settlement. It is the Holy City, revered by the world's three major monotheistic religions. And it is a Golden City of narrow lanes and magnificent sweeping vistas. But Jerusalem is also a city of the late twentieth century and, like every other city in this decade, it has a special pace and a host of problems. If the visitor sees only one of these Jerusalems, he has not experienced Jerusalem.

To capture the flavor of any city in the world, the visitor must walk endlessly. You must be willing to stray off the beaten path and into side alleys and walled courtyards, places that the ordinary tourist rarely sees. You must allow every one of your senses to range freely   to touch, to smell, to listen, to talk to everyone and anyone, to imagine and to re-create. And you must do it either alone or with one or two friends, at most, for there is nothing more discouraging to the meaningful chance encounter than a horde of picture-snapping tourists marching down the street.

Of all cities, Jerusalem in particular is open only to those with strong legs. It grew by neighborhoods, and each neighborhood preserves its own traditional way of life. The variety cannot be grasped by the casual passerby. On foot, you can see not only the beautiful side of the city, but its ugly and depressing places as well. These are as much a part of the life of this city as are the sections decked out in their Sabbath best. And the real beauty of Jerusalem is not the noble building spotted here and there but the twist down an ancient closed lane that suddenly, unexpectedly, opens onto a breadth of mountains and valleys.

This guidebook describes eight walking tours through the familiar and unfamiliar sections of the city. A stop point has been indicated in the middle of most of the walks to enable the weary to call it a day and find another occasion to pick up where they left off. Each step of the way has been plotted and mapped, for even the native Jerusalemite has difficulty navigating through some of the older neighborhoods. Each presents a composite picture of the city: a bit of the old and some of the new; at least one immigrant community that retains a way of life quite different from its surroundings; people at work, from the baker at his open hearth to the craftsman in a modern workshop; a well-to-do neighborhood — facing a slum area; a declivity in the topography that served King Solomon's water-carrier system even as it served the Israeli soldiers in the 1948 War of Independence.

As you walk through Jerusalem, it will become increasingly clear that the life and shape of the city has been fashioned by five constantly recurring themes:

Water — where to find it, how to conserve it in time of peace, how to protect it in time of war.

Defense walls — they must be built everywhere and they must be formidable; if they fail, a second, third and fourth line of defense must be planned; no detail in the defensive system can be left to chance, from the way in which a door is to be opened to the form and placement of a major arsenal.

Stones — a veritable passion for every stony corner. Archaeologists turn each one over carefully for a clue as to when it was used. Each conqueror of Jerusalem breaks apart the stones of a former reign and uses them again to rebuild Jerusalem in his own image. Each master builder leaves his signature on the very face of the stones, from King Herod with his two-ton blocks elegantly indented on all sides, to the twelfth-century mason whose wages were calculated by the number of stones bearing his personal mark.

Foreigners — immigrants, pilgrims, visitors, conquerors, all must somehow learn to share one beloved place in one hundred different ways. The "melting pot" theory never took hold here, and this remains the city's most difficult problem and the source of its centuries'-old appeal.

Three Religions — Moslem, Christian and Jewish — claim Jerusalem as their own. The unmistakable costumes of each religious group identify its adherents at one glance, and each group protects its rights with jealous concern. In this theme, preceding ones meet and merge. The stones of almost every holy place are meaningful not to one but to three. And the waters of the Shiloah cleansed the priests of the Second Temple; they were blessed in the early churches on the Holy Mount; and they washed the faithful at the Dome of the Rock.

There is no other city in the world that offers so much to so many different people. You, among them, may find something that cannot be found elsewhere.

DATES TO REMEMBER

FROM KING DAVID TO THE SIX-DAY WAR

THE CANAANITE PERIOD 3000-1200 B.C.

2100 B.C. In the days of the Patriarch Abraham Jerusalem was governed by the Canaanite King Melchizedek, described in Chapter XIV of *Genesis* as "King of Salem."

1400 B.C. Jerusalem is mentioned as the principal town of Canaan in the Tel el-Amarna letters, a dispatch to Egypt warning of the approach of tribes from the East.

1300 B.C. The Israelites enter the Promised Land and the kings of the mountains and the plains band together to fight the "tribes from the East."

THE FIRST TEMPLE PERIOD 1200-586 B.C.

1000 B.C. King David conquers the city from the Jebusites, brings the Ark of the Covenant to Jerusalem and buys a threshing floor from Araunah the Jebusite to use for an altar to the Lord. By this act, he sets in motion the process that converts this place into the Holy City.

960 B.C. King Solomon builds the First Temple and launches a vast building program. He signs pacts with the neighboring kings and Jerusalem becomes, for the first time, a city of international reknown.

922 B.C. The City is besieged and plundered by Shishak, Pharoah of Egypt.

700 B.C.   Sennacherib, the Assyrian leader, "with his cohorts all gleaming in purple and gold," besieges Jerusalem and King Hezekiah of Judah protects the city water supply by building an extraordinary tunnel from the water source outside the city walls to a reservoir inside the city.

687 B.C.   Hezekiah's son, King Menasseh, repairs the city that had been ravaged during the Assyrian siege.

600 B.C.   The city grows toward the west and new walls encompass the Upper City: Mount Zion and the area now occupied by the Jewish Quarter.

586 B.C.   Nebuchadnezzar, King of Babylon, destroys the city and the Temple. The people are led into captivity, where "by the waters of Babylon they sat down and wept as they remembered Zion." This was the end of sovereign Jewish rule of Jerusalem till 164 B.C.

THE SECOND TEMPLE PERIOD 536 B.C.-70 A.D.

536 B.C.   The Babylonian Exile continues for fifty years. Cyrus, King of Persia, allows the people to return to Jerusalem.

515 B.C.   The Temple is rehabilitated.

444 B.C.   Nehemiah, Governor of Judah, rebuilds the wall of Jerusalem in 52 days and organizes the immigrants into a "new society."

332 B.C.   Alexander the Great conquers the Fertile Crescent and Jerusalem changes hands without a battle. After his death the city is given to the Ptolemies and it is besieged once again, this time on the Sabbath when no resistance can be made.

198 B.C.   Jerusalem is conquered by Antiochus III and the cruel Seleucid dynasty of Hellenist Syria dominates Jerusalem for the next thirty years.

170 B.C.   Antiochus IV Epiphanes enters the city to deal with unrest among the natives. By desecrating the Temple, he evokes a rebellion led by the Maccabees.

164 B.C.   Judah Maccabee takes Jerusalem and cleanses the Temple in the first celebration of Hannukah, the Festival of Lights. Sovereign Jewish rule of the city continues for a century.

153 B.C.   The Maccabees found a dynasty of priest-kings, the Has-
           moneans. They manage to produce a number of famous
           rulers — Salome, Alexander Jannaeus, Aristobulus — who,
           although quite busy fighting amongst themselves, have
           enough time and energy left over to completely sever Syrian
           influence in the Holy Land.

63 B.C.   Pompey, leading an army of Roman Legionnaires, conquers
           Jerusalem and dismantles its walls and fortifications. This
           date marks the end of sovereign Jewish rule of Jerusalem
           till it is restored in 1948 A.D. with the declaration of the
           State of Israel. Herod the Great is appointed King by the
           Roman Senate and rules for thirty-three years. In the
           great tradition of barbarian kings he kills off quite a large
           number of family members, but as master builder of
           Jerusalem he makes his capital the most splendid city in
           the Middle East. Ten thousand builders and one thousand
           priests toil to build Herod's Temple. One thousand char-
           iots haul the building materials. It takes eight years to
           finish the courtyard and the colonnades. Josephus describes
           the king's palace as "baffling all description"; the rebuilt
           and new walls with their 150 towers as "square and solid as
           the wall itself, and in the joining and the beauty of the
           stones in no wise inferior to a temple"; the towers of the
           Citadel whose stones were "so nicely joined" to one another
           that each tower seemed like one natural rock, and the aque-
           duct that "at immense expense" brought an "abundant
           supply of water from a distance and provided an easy ascent
           by two hundred steps of the purest white marble." Jerusalem
           is entirely rebuilt during the Herodian reign.

4 B.C.   Roman procurators rule Jerusalem for the next seventy-
           four years, with a brief break for King Agrippa I.

33 A.D.   It is Herod's splendid Jerusalem that draws Jesus again and
           again, until the Crucifixion, ordered by the fifth Roman
           Procurator, Pontius Pilate.

66   Oppressed by the Roman procurators, the first Jewish revolt
           against Rome begins.

70   The revolt is crushed. Jerusalem is taken by Titus and the
           Second Temple is destroyed in a great conflagration. Titus'

Arch, in Rome, shows the people being led to slavery and Roman soldiers bearing the Menorah which they had looted from the ruins of the Temple.

THE ROMAN PERIOD 70-324 A.D.

132   Emperor Hadrian tries to turn Jerusalem into a pagan city and thereby incites the Bar Kochba rebellion.

135   The rebellion is crushed and Jerusalem becomes Aelia Capitolina, a typical Roman garrison town, with a temple to Venus and a statue of Jupiter adorning the Temple Mount.

THE BYZANTINE PERIOD 324-638 A.D.

324   Jerusalem has become central to a rising Christianity. Constantine the Great and his mother Queen Helene identify holy sites and crown them with magnificent churches. The majority of the population is Christian.

333   The Traveler of Bordeaux speaks of that stone on the Temple Mount where Jews are allowed to pray on the ninth day of the Hebrew month of Av, the date that the First and Second Temple were destroyed and the only day of the year on which they are allowed to enter the city.

362   The Emperor Julian promises that he will rebuild the Sanctuary on the Temple Mount, but a mysterious fire breaks out during the early stages of building and the project is brought to an abrupt halt.

443   The Empress Eudocia establishes a new air of tolerance; a call for immigration from the Diaspora brings Jewish settlers.

614   The Persians conquer Jerusalem, destroy the churches and murder the inhabitants.

629   The Persians are driven out by Emperor Heraclius, but Islam, the next invader, will take over in less than ten years.

THE MOSLEM PERIOD 638-1099 A.D.

638 The city falls to the army of the Caliph Omar and Jerusalem becomes the third city in Islam, after Mecca and Medina. Omar, an unusually tolerant monarch, allows adherents of all faiths to reside in the City, giving them all equal rights. He declares that the Moslems had come to the country because they were kinsmen of the Israelites, both groups having traced their ancestry to a single common father, Abraham.

697 Abd el Malik completes construction of the Dome of the Rock as a monument to mark the place where the Prophet Mohammed was carried on his Night Journey. His elder son al-Walid builds the Mosque of Al-Aksa beside it as a place to celebrate festive occasions for the Moslems of Syria and Palestine, who could not manage the lengthy journey to far-off Mecca.

969 Jerusalem, which was ruled benevolently by the Damascus-based Umayyad Caliphate till 750 A.D. and by the Baghdad-based and neglectful Abbasid Caliphate for the next two centuries, falls to al-Hakim, the Fatimid despot of Egypt who orders the destruction of all synagogues and churches in the City.

1071 The city is conquered by the Seljuk Turks in an assault of unbridled devastation. Christian pilgrims are banned from Jerusalem and the outraged European Christians begin to prepare for the Crusades.

THE CRUSADER PERIOD 1099-1250 A.D.

1099 Godfrey de Bouillon captures Jerusalem, slaughtering Moslems and Jews indiscriminately and setting fire to the Jewish Quarter, which was then situated to the north of the Temple Mount. The Crusaders ban Jewish and Moslem settlements in the city as profane. They rebuild the churches, establish hospitals and hospices for Christian pilgrims and even a gigantic currency exchange which still stands on the Via Dolorosa.

1170   Benjamin of Tudela visits Jerusalem and reports that "there is a dye-factory there, which the Jews rent yearly from the king, so that no man but the Jews shall do any dying work in Jerusalem, and there are about 200 Jews living below the Tower of David at the limits of the (city) State."

1187   Sultan Saladin expels the Crusaders and, mindful of the Jews who had fought alongside the Arabs to retake Jerusalem, gives them the right to live in the City.

THE MAMELUKES 1250-1517 A.D.

1250   A mysterious group of slave-kings, the Mamelukes rule Jerusalem from Cairo and it becomes once again a provincial city. In the course of the two and a half centuries of their rule the city is subject to earthquakes, epidemics, drought, locust plagues, famine and persecution by the local emirs. Jews are forced to wear yellow turbans, Samaritans red ones and Christians blue. Only Moslem turbans are white. But the Mamelukes contribute a treasure of magnificent Islamic buildings to the glory of Jerusalem.

1492   The Jews are expelled from Spain and many find their way to Jerusalem.

1493   The Ottoman conquest of Constantinople signals the end of the Byzantine Empire and in a short time Jerusalem will begin four hundred years of Turkish rule.

THE OTTOMAN PERIOD 1516-1917 A.D.

1517   Palestine and Jerusalem become a part of the Ottoman Empire.

1537   Sultan Suleiman the Magnificent repairs and rebuilds the walls and gates of Jerusalem that confine the Old City today. He restores the Citadel and improves the city's water supply. But Jerusalem remains a backwater town throughout the Ottoman period.

1799   Napoleon lands in Acre. His plans for a siege of Jerusalem are never realized and Jerusalem loses its most interesting potential ruler.

1831   A brief respite from Turkish rule is won by Mohammed Ali
        of Egypt who introduces a touch of modernity and a notion
        of tolerance. It is at this time that the Hurva Synagogue,
        built in 1700 and destroyed by the Arabs in 1721, is rebuilt.
1855   The Sultan of Turkey grants permission for non-Moslems to
        enter the Temple Mount and institutes an era of religious
        tolerance.
1860   Sir Moses Montefiore, after paying his first visit to Palestine,
        funds the construction of the first Jewish Quarter outside
        the city wall. A new period of concerted construction of
        educational institutions, churches, synagogues, schools and
        convents begins.
1892   The Jerusalem-Jaffa line, one of the earliest railways in the
        Middle East, has its first run.

THE BRITISH MANDATORY PERIOD 1917-1948 A.D.

1917   The English, at war with the Germans and their allies the
        Turks, issue the Balfour Declaration which promises the
        Jews a national home in Palestine. One month later, in
        December, a victorious General Allenby enters Jerusalem
        and Ottoman rule in Palestine comes to an end.
1920   Sir Herbert Samuel becomes the First High Commissioner of
        Palestine, with his office established in Jerusalem. The
        killing of eight Jews near the Western Wall marks the
        beginning of the violence that is to characterize the rela-
        tions between Jewish and Arab residents at frequent inter-
        vals during the next twenty-eight years.
1922   A British mandate to rule Palestine is approved by the
        League of Nations. Sir Patrick Geddes, the greatest of
        English town planners, is brought to Jerusalem and decides
        that Mount Scopus will be the home of the Hebrew
        University.
1947   The United Nations decides to partition Palestine between
        Arabs and Jews and declares a *corpus separatum*, or inter-
        national administration for Jerusalem at least for a period of
        ten years.

1948   Explosions on Ben Yehudah Street, in the courtyard of the
              Jewish Agency building and in the offices of **The Palestine
              Post** are the precursors of the war that will soon begin.

JERUSALEM DIVIDED AND REUNITED 1948-1967 A.D.

1948   The British Mandate ends and Israel's War of Independence
              begins the following day, May 15. There are battles
              throughout the city. When the fighting ends Jerusalem is
              partitioned: the western and southern neighborhoods to
              Israel; the Old City, with the holy places of the three mono-
              theistic faiths, and the neighborhoods to the east, to the
              Arabs. A wall divides the city in two.
1949   Prime Minister Ben-Gurion proclaims Jerusalem as the
              capital of Israel. The Arab section is ruled by the Hashe-
              mite Kingdom of Jordan.
1967...   During the Six-Day War Israeli soldiers enter the Old City.
              The dividing wall is demolished and the Old City and its
              suburbs are annexed to Jerusalem. A new cycle of growth,
              construction and prosperity begins...

TIPS FOR WALKERS

1. Avoid being outdoors for any length of time in the high-noon sun — between one and three in the afternoon. The short introduction to each walk will usually tell you the best time to start out.

2. Keep your head covered at all times. Between the months of May and October the Israeli sun burns fiercely.

3. Don't burden yourself by taking along snacks. There isn't a neighborhood in Jerusalem without its own kiosk. You may get tired of the beigelach (doughnut-shaped bread roll) they supply, but buy them anyhow, if only for the opportunity of talking to the owner.

4. Drink bottled soda or juice frequently!

5. Dress comfortably but modestly. You will be entering neighborhoods where short, short skirts and bare arms are frowned upon. If you have taken note of Tip 2, above, a headcovering will already be handy, as needed, when you enter some of the churches and synagogues mentioned in the walks. An extra scarf will do to cover bare arms.

6. Tuck a candle and matches in your bag. Some of the caves and grottoes you will be visiting do not have windows or electricity.

7. You might want to take along a small, handled, string or plastic bag, for something may strike your fancy as you walk through the streets and if you don't acquire it immediately you may never be able to find it again.

8. Camera addicts should try their best to leave the beloved instrument at home. Hundreds of good shots will suggest themselves on each walk. Pick out the best ones, examine them from all angles, and return some other time when you can give all your attention to photography.

9. For any walk that takes longer than two hours to complete, a midway point is noted at a place convenient to public transportation. You may stop there and return some other time to finish the walk.

10. If, on the other hand, you have inordinate energy, you may do one and a half or two walks at one go. Some walks end close to where another begins.

11. All place names and streets are written in bold-face type so that you can find your place in the text after you have taken time out for finding your place on the street. These place names appear on the accompanying map for each walk.

THE FIRST WALK

FROM THE MOUNT OF OLIVES
TO THE WATERS OF ROGEL

Jerusalem is one of the few cities on earth that has been inhabited continuously for thousands of years. On this walk you will see how Jerusalem grew in its first twelve hundred years of recorded history from a tiny enclave of Jebusites on Mount Ophel to a city of splendor with 100,000 people in the first century A.D. (Today, the population of Jerusalem is almost four times greater than it was then.) This walk starts at the top of the Mount of Olives, perhaps the most famous of all the mountains surrounding Jerusalem. The footpaths of Olivet descend into the Kidron Valley, taking you to the site of the first Jerusalem, the city that King David conquered from the Jebusites and made into the capital of his kingdom. With King Solomon's building of the First Temple on the adjacent hill, Mount Moriah, where, according to tradition, Abraham was commanded to sacrifice his beloved son Isaac, the city spread northward. The walls surrounding Mount Moriah today were the contribution of King Herod in yet a later period of Jerusalem's development. Since the Jerusalem you will see on this walk is the Jerusalem of the Bible, take one along to check the references. You will need both the Old and the New Testaments.

The walk looks treacherous but is in fact quite easy to manage since it is downhill all the way. There is only one street sign to guide you, so take along one or more partners, preferably those among your acquaintances who have proven talents in direction-finding and landmark-spotting. Don't try

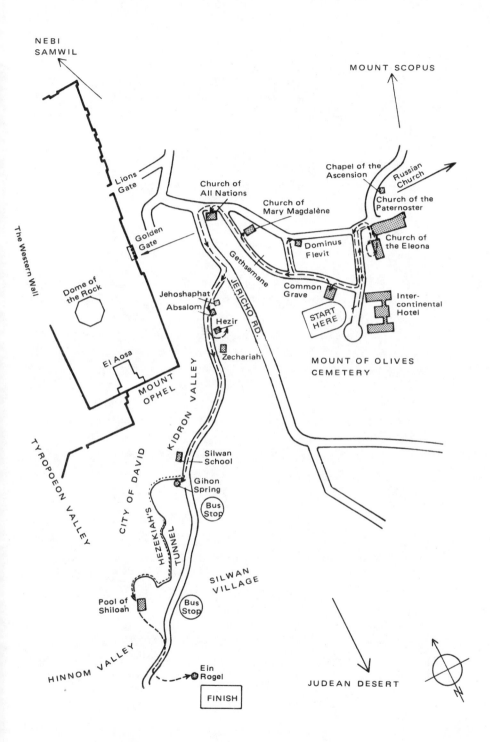

NEBI
SAMWIL

MOUNT SCOPUS

The Western Wall

Lions
Gate

Church of
All Nations

Chapel of the
Ascension

Russian
Church

Church of
Mary Magdalène

Church of the
Paternoster

Golden
Gate

Dominus
Flevit

Church of
the Eleona

Dome of
the Rock

Gethsemane

JERICHO RD.

Jehoshaphat

Common
Grave

Inter-
continental
Hotel

Absalom

El Aqsa

Hezir

START
HERE

Zechariah

MOUNT
OPHEL

MOUNT OF OLIVES
CEMETERY

KIDRON VALLEY

CITY OF DAVID

TYROPOEON VALLEY

Silwan
School

Gihon
Spring

Bus
Stop

HEZEKIAH'S TUNNEL

SILWAN
VILLAGE

Pool of
Shiloah

Bus
Stop

HINNOM VALLEY

Ein
Rogel

JUDEAN DESERT

FINISH

N

it on Sunday or between the hours of twelve and two when
many of the churches on the Mount of Olives are closed. It's
a fine walk for Saturday because it doesn't pass a single
commercial area and public transportation is provided by the
Arab bus system which operates seven days a week. Clothes:
the most comfortable you possess; shoes: with rubber soles.
If you are adventurous, wear a bathing suit underneath your
street clothes so that you can wade through Hezekiah's Tun-
nel — purely optional.

This walk begins at the **Intercontinental Hotel,** which can be reached
via taxi or the No. 42 bus coming from the Central Bus Station. For
the best observation point, stand at the edge of the road just below
the hotel. This part of the **Mount of Olives** can be seen from almost any
spot in Jerusalem and anyone standing on it can see the entire city. On
a clear day you can see forever — or at least as far as **Nebi Samwil,** the
rise that Richard the Lion-Hearted called the Mount of Joy because it
was from there that he got his first glimpse of Jerusalem as he
approached it from the northwest. You are standing southeast of Nebi
Samwil so look for it on the horizon to your left.

Just ahead of you is the walled city of Jerusalem. This view of the
Old City, with the golden **Dome of the Rock** dominating the foreground, can be found on the walls of countless travel bureaus, but what
picture can do justice to a sight such as this!

Look for the southeast corner of the Old City Wall and of the Temple Wall — they are one and the same at this point. From this corner the
wall cuts to the west, moves south again, and cuts to the west once
more. In the space made by this angle there is a large open space bordered by a curving road. From here, the open space appears to be a
jumble of rocks, but if you look with a discerning eye you can make
out a wide staircase that led the residents of the City of David up to the
Second Temple built some two thousand years ago. This monumental
staircase was uncovered in the course of a nine-year dig, concluded in
1977, at the foot of the Temple Mount. Immediately south of the curving road there is a settlement on top of a sloping cliff. This settlement
was once the **City of David,** built upon **Mount Ophel** and occupied

*A bygone view of Nebi Samwil from
the Mount of Olives*

since prehistoric times. That's all there was to the Jerusalem of the Bible. You will notice that Mount Ophel is not as high as many of its surrounding mountains; its sense of security came from the fact that it was surrounded on three sides by deep valleys.

Now look into the Temple Mount itself. This is really a man-made plateau; the level of the ground inside the walls of the Mount is much higher than the level outside. If you look at the courtyard in front of the silver-domed El Aqsa Mosque you can see that the Wall rises only about four yards above ground level within the Mount. You can also see that the Wall is actually much higher here than elsewhere. Elsewhere, the lower courses of the Wall are buried below the valley floor. It is estimated that the Wall is 48 yards high. Why were these huge walls necessary? When King Herod decided to rebuild the Second Temple, he was determined to make it one of the showplaces of the known world. But his vision was constrained by the known dimensions of the First Temple which had, over the centuries, become sanctified and could not be changed, even to suit the dreams of empire-builders. According to the prescribed dimensions, which were later codified in the *Mishnah*, the Temple fitted neatly into a small area in the center of the Temple Mount, approximately at the place where the golden Dome of the Rock now stands. (Nobody knows exactly where.) The land to the south of that site sloped down to meet the level of the Mount of Ophel while the land to the north climbed higher. Since the size of the Temple was limited, King Herod decided to build a mighty platform to set off the relatively small Temple. It was the platform that would show the world his talents as a master builder. He ordered that the mountain rising north of the Temple site be levelled and, in a huge land-fill operation — minus bulldozers — poured the top of the mountain onto the lower slope lying to the south of the Temple. The Herodian wall is, therefore, a huge retaining wall that keeps the artificial mountain from tumbling down into the Kidron Valley. The southeast corner of the Wall is the strongest corner of the entire circuit since it must bear the bulk of the land pressure. The lower 44 yards of wall are genuine Herodian Wall; the upper 4 yards were built and rebuilt by successive conquerors.

Only a small portion of the Temple Mount area stretching out before you is considered holy ground; the rest of the area surrounding the site of the Temple itself was used for functions not considered "holy," such as money-changing for pilgrims coming from distant lands.

As you face the Old City, look to your far left to see how close Jerusalem is to the desert. The **Judean Desert,** unlike the Desert of Sinai where human beings can survive only if they remain close to an oasis, has always been able to sustain wandering tribes. But the needs of nomads often conflicted with the city's propertied settlers — particularly in years of drought when the nomads became desperate for water for themselves and their flocks. The isolated urbanists in the City of David built thick walls around their settlement to protect themselves. The Turks were wont to kill a few desert nomads every so often in order to discourage their predatory instincts. For national leaders who found themselves in precarious political situations, the desert served as a temporary home. There they could keep watch over political developments until the time was ripe to return to their source of power in the city. This happened to King David: you will read his story when you reach **Absalom's Memorial,** whose coned top you can see among the trees in the valley directly below the golden dome. It was to this wilderness that the saints of the New Testament went, either to escape from religious persecution or to strengthen their resolve.

As you look out over the cityscape from this vantage point a few more facts about Jerusalem's geographic situation become clear. First, Jerusalem is a city whose shape has been determined by its valleys: the **Kidron,** below you; the **Hinnom,** which borders the west side of the city and swings to the east to meet the Kidron (you can see it as a deep cleft in the ground south of the City of David); the **Tyropoeon Valley** that cuts through the center of the Old City and continues southward to form the western boundary of the City of David. It ends where the other two valleys meet. Because it has been filled in over the centuries the Tyropoeon can't be seen too clearly today, but you will know where it lies by identifying the buildings which rise upward to the top of a mountain ridge to the west of it. This is **Mount Zion,** the Upper City of the Second Temple Era, where kings and princes built their palaces and pleasure gardens. The courtiers reached the Temple Mount via graceful bridges that spanned the Tyropoeon.

On a high point on the southern horizon to your left there is a wooded area that shelters the United Nations Command Headquarters. In Biblical times this place was referred to as the **Hill of Evil Counsel,** an appelation which may appear to be still suitable.

Most of the tall towers on the western horizon were added to the traditional Jerusalem skyline in the building boom of the 1970's. Looking from left to right you see the **Omariya Apartment Building**, the **Dormition Church** on Mount Zion with its black-coned top and adjoining tower, the massive, broad, many-windowed **King David Hotel**, the graceful tower of the **Y.M.C.A.**, and two new commercial towers in the central business district.

The Intercontinental Hotel is fine for tourists who want the best possible view at all times, but one achingly wonders whether some other, less commercial venture might not have better preserved the age-old glory of this revered mountain. If you haven't had your morning coffee yet, you might as well benefit from the spoilage of the Mount and have a cupful served in the hotel's glassed-in lounge. On a comfortable sofa you can continue to read about the Mount of Olives and enjoy the glorious view.

The ancient and gnarled olive trees that gave the mountain its name stand either alone or in clusters along the entire slope of the mountain. Olive trees have been growing on this mountain for some 3,000 **years.** The mountain is mentioned for the first time in the *Book of Samuel II*, 15:30: "David went up the ascent of the Mount of Olives, weeping as he went, barefoot and with his head covered," as he mourned his betrayal by his favorite son, Absalom.

The Mount of Olives was also famous as a burning calendar. Long ago, when Jews were exiled from their country and dispersed throughout the Middle East, they relied on the learned men remaining in Jerusalem to inform them of the exact dates of the holidays they were to celebrate in the Diaspora. The Jewish calendar is based on the lunar month; when the new moon appeared in Jerusalem a huge bonfire was built on the top of the Mount of Olives. Mountaintop outposts were designated throughout the areas in which Jews resided; when the first outpost saw the fire on the Mount of Olives, its own bonfire was lit, and similarly down the line, until a string of blazing mountaintops extended throughout the entire area where Jews lived.

Stretching down the mountainside as far as the eye can see are rows and rows of gravestones. The slope is a vast necropolis. The oldest graves here are from the Bronze Age and some of the new ones hold Ministers of the State of Israel. Hundreds of generations of Jews, from lowly water-carriers to renowned scholars, have been buried on the Mount to await the Day of Judgement, for it is written in the *Book of Joel*: "For behold, in those days and at that time, when I restore the fortunes of Judah and Jerusalem, I will gather all the nations and bring them down to the valley of Jehoshaphat, and I will enter into Judgement with them there, on account of my people, and my heritage Israel, because they have scattered them among the nations and have divided up my land..." The section of the Kidron Valley that borders the Mount of Olives has traditionally been known as the **Valley of Jehoshaphat**, which means, "the Lord will judge." The prophet Zechariah, too, foresees that Great Day: "On that day His feet shall stand on the Mount of Olives which lies before Jerusalem on the east...and the whole land shall be turned into a plain but Jerusalem shall remain aloft upon its site...and it shall be inhabited, for there shall be no more destruction; Jerusalem shall dwell in security."

According to an old Jewish tradition, when the Messiah arrives a *shofar* (ram's horn) will be blown from the Temple Mount. Those who are buried far away, in distant lands, will have to roll through the earth in order to reach the Mount of Olives because the inhabitants of its graves will be the first to enter Paradise. It is preferable to be buried at the right spot from the start.

Closed to Jewish visitors throughout the 19 years when the city was divided, the cemetery suffered extensive damage during its period of abandonment. Some of the old headstones were even incorporated into the road leading into the hotel. The records of the Jewish Burial Society have been combed to find the exact location of vanished graves and an extensive program of restoration is underway.

When you leave the hotel follow the road on your right. It is the only paved road on the mountain and connects the Mount of Olives with its neighbor to the north, **Mount Scopus**. As you walk along this road, groups of little boys may suddenly appear, as if from out of the olive trees. They will offer their services as guides. Do not naively assume that a small tip will make them disappear; it will only inspire them to bring out all their brothers and cousins to share in the bounty.

In a block or so the road will veer to the right and just around the bend and a little way up the hill you will come upon the iron gate that leads into both the **Church of the Eleona** and the **Church of the Paternoster**. The gate is open from 8:30 to 11:30 and from 3 to 4:30. Beyond the gateway, turn right and in a few steps you will be in the outer courtyard of Eleona, originally built by Constantine in the fourth century. Emperor Constantine was interested in three major sites in the history of Jesus' sojourn on earth and considered them all to be of equal significance: the place of Jesus' birth, which Constantine memorialized in the Church of the Nativity in Bethlehem; the place of his burial, in the Church of the Holy Sepulchre in Jerusalem; and the place where he "revealed to his disciples inscrutable mysteries," in the Church of the Eleona. The first two churches retained their extraordinary significance throughout the centuries. Only Eleona disappeared without a trace, until excavations in 1910 brought it to light once again. All that remained were the bare outlines of the original Byzantine church.

The open space in which you are standing is the atrium, where worshippers could assemble before the service. They were protected from the harsh sun by a stone roof supported by a rectangle of pillars. The long narrow platform bordering the entrance to the church proper is the narthex, where those who were in the process of converting to Christianity could remain during services; they were not allowed to enter the church until they had completed all their studies. You will see the church itself as you continue the walk.

Now, retrace your steps past the iron entrance gate. Directly ahead is the **Church of the Paternoster** established by Queen Helene, Constantine's mother. She was the Emperor's major partner in changing the Jerusalem landscape from pagan to Christian. She came to Jerusalem to build churches on the places where significant events in the life of Jesus took place. Her final decisions are considered authoritative if only because her monuments were built in a period relatively close to the time at which the events were recorded.

Each church on the Mount of Olives relates to an event that occurred on Jesus' last pilgrimage to Jerusalem, when he and his disciples came to celebrate the Passover festival. They gathered at Bethphage, or Bethany, now part of a little Arab village that lies on the eastern slope of the Mount of Olives. Together they made their way to the top of the mountain, stopping here and there for rest. Where you are now was the resting place where Jesus taught his students the Credo (*paternoster* in Latin) — "Our Father, which art in heaven." Throughout the stone corridors of the church there are little niches, and in each niche is a rendition of the Credo in another language. Look for the Hebrew and the Arabic versions of the paternoster. They are both on the same wall, separated only by the Armenians. National alliances are constantly changing, but here all nations' positions are permanent.

No user of this book would even entertain the idea of writing his name on the stones of this church, as did so many non-users!

At the far end of the inner courtyard you will find a staircase next to the French paternoster that leads into the Church of the Eleona proper. Reconstruction of this church has only recently been completed and all its stones are new or salvaged. The only ones remaining from the original church can be found on either side of the altar. No superfluous ornamentation mars the pure form of the church, which was divided into three aisles by two rows of pillars. The pillars you see today are not the original ones; all that remains of the originals are the stone squares set into the ground upon which the genuine Byzantine pillars once rested. To the left of the altar is a small patch of the original mosaic floor, now enclosed in a border of new and inappropriate bricks. Wet the mosaics a bit to make the natural blues, rusts and greens of the native stone stand out clearly. Each piece is painstakingly chiseled by hand into the pattern designed by the anonymous fourth-century artisan.

Leave the churches and look behind you at the **Tower of the Russian Church** which you will see again and again from many different vantage points on these walks, but this is the closest you shall come to it. Just opposite to where you are now standing is the **Church of the Ascension,** marked by a small dome and minaret. You need not enter the church; merely note that the minaret on a Christian holy place is typical of religious sites in this city, where a holy site is often claimed by at least two, if not three, of Jerusalem's religious groups.

Retrace your steps in the direction of the Intercontinental and shortly, at a sign reading "Common Grave of the Fallen of the Old City," you will find a staircase leading down the Mount of Olives. On the right of the staircase you can clearly see the broken remains of violated Jewish graves. On the left there is a sign announcing that this is the burial place of the Prophets Haggai, Malachi and Zechariah. Notice the Cyrilic inscription on the stone gateposts. Up until 1948 this burial lot was owned and cared for by members of the Russian Church. Today's attendant and his family live on the grounds and he will be pleased to show you around the darkly mysterious circular aisles that lead between the burial niches carved into the rocks.

Further down the stairs and also on the left you will come upon the **Common Grave** of all those who fell in the battle for the Jewish Quarter during the 1948 War of Independence. Their remains were found only after the Six-Day War and were brought to the Mount of Olives for reburial. Even if you do not read Hebrew you can read the ages of those

who fell, among them boys who were very very young. These youngsters delivered messages between the various outposts. Notice that
although they were never part of the organized defense forces they have
been accorded the status of fallen soldiers and have been assigned Army
identification numbers.

Continue the mountain descent. This path, according to tradition, is
the one Jesus followed on his last pilgrimage into Jerusalem; it is still
taken by Catholic pilgrims every Palm Sunday. The path is no longer
stony and broken, as it must have been then, but it descends sharply so
walk carefully.

The thrust of the Temple Mount Wall you see before you was seen
by all who followed this descent from the beginning of the Common
Era, when the wall was built. Before that, in 900 B.C., pilgrims looking
into the Temple Mount from this path would have seen King Solomon's
First Temple; in 400 B.C. they would have seen Ezra and Nehemiah's
version of the Second Temple; in 4 B.C. King Herod's Second Temple;
in 150 A.D. Hadrian's Roman temple to the gods, and finally, from
697 A.D., the golden Dome of the Rock, built at the beginning of Moslem rule in Jerusalem.

As you descend Olivet, you will see, off to your right, the black and
white "art nouveau" **Basilica of Dominus Flevit,** which means, literally,
"the Lord wept." "And when he drew near and saw the city he wept
over it, saying, 'Would that even today you knew the things that make
for peace... For the days shall come upon you, when your enemies will
cast up a bank about you and surround you, and hem you in on every
side, and dash you to the ground, you and your children within you,
and they will not leave one stone upon another...'" (*Luke,* 20:41). This
is an accurate description of what indeed did happen to Jerusalem at
the hands of the Romans, a few decades later.

Visiting hours are from 8:30 to 11:30 and 3 to 6. If you arrive
during non-visiting hours, try pulling the bell rope outside the great iron
gate of the church and one of the Franciscan fathers will come to show
you through the grounds. You will see remnants of a necropolis which
began in the Middle Bronze Age, the period in which King David conquered the Jebusite city, as well as heavily ornamented ossuaries of the
Second Temple period. Most important, you will see the lovely basilica,
the work of the church architect Barluzzi, who understood the potential of his site and designed the church window as a picture frame
around the view of the Old City. He wisely integrated the patches

of mosaics left from the Byzantine church into the floor of the new church.

After your visit to Dominus Flevit, continue walking down the Mount of Olives. The road passes between high stone walls. The Mount of Olives is divided among the various religions, and further divided among orders within each religion. Every group and subgroup jealously guards its property rights on the mountain by encircling its own domain with high stone walls. The wall on your left separates the Jewish property from the Christian property, defined by the wall on your right.

At one point the road forks. Your path is the one on the right. This is one of the most beautiful pathways in all Jerusalem. Each twist in the road opens up a new view. Look straight up at five of the seven onion domes of the Russian **Church of Mary Magdaléne.** At the next twist you will be looking down onto the many-domed roof of the **Church of All Nations.**

You are now walking beside the famous **Gardens of Gethsemane,** noted in the New Testament as the place where Jesus often met to study with his disciples. Gethsemane means "olive oil press," the kind that you will be able to examine at the Agricultural Museum on your Fifth Walk.

The stone rollers that squash the olives were often cut from the rock on the same spot where they were to be used; sometimes they remained lying in place for centuries after the grove which supplied the olives had been cut down. Up until the turn of the century, you could still see the old circular stones in the gardens of Gethsemane.

A bit further down the road is the entrance to the Church of Mary Magdaléne, built in 1888 by the Russian Emperor Alexander III. (There is a token entrance fee.) A map of the Holy Land prepared in the same period shows all of Jerusalem's holy buildings topped with domes subtly changed in form to resemble the onion shapes on this church. Rest on one of the benches in the Church gardens. This is a fine time to open the New Testament section of your Bible and review the story of Jesus' last pilgrimage to Jerusalem. Of particular interest to Jewish visitors will be the threads of Jewish law and custom woven into the story and the description of the religious life of the city during the period of the Second Temple. The report is given by those who were dismayed by what they saw, but considered themselves, at least at that time, members of the "loyal opposition."

Leave the Russian Church gardens and continue along the same path until you come to a bona fide street. Turn left and in a few paces you will come to an iron door in the wall on your left. This is the only entrance to the **Church of All Nations**, though its impressive facade might invite the uninitiated to enter from the main road. This side entrance to the church leads into another section of the Gardens of Gethsemane. It contains eight ancient olive trees. The Franciscans, who own this church, claim that "it is historically certain that these trees have existed for over thirteen centuries; for they have never been subject to the tax which is levied upon all newly planted trees since the Moslem conquest (in 638)." This is the place where Jesus spent a night of agony, knowing that in the morning he would be betrayed by one of his own disciples. The church was built on the remains of another Byzantine church, with funds contributed by "all the nations." Every effort has been made to recapture the Byzantine form, even to the repetition of the patterns in the original floor, parts of which can be seen through a protective glass covering.

When you leave the Church of All Nations through its garden entrance, turn left. After what can only have been a shoe-damaging descent down the Mount of Olives you deserve a short stretch on the modern highway that passes in front of the church. It was built by King Hussein on one of the most ancient of roadbeds — the Route to Jericho.

Cross **Jericho Road,** carefully, for a better view of the facade of the Church of All Nations with its famous glowing tympanum, depicting Jesus' acceptance of the sorrows of the world.

From the point where you are now standing there is a clear view of the Moslem cemetery that borders the whole length of the eastern wall of the Old City. The graves of the poor *fellahin* are marked by a simple circle of stones. Notice the century plants growing in the center of a number of these circles. The name of this plant "sabr" (not to be confused with the cactus whose name is used to characterize the native-born Israeli sabrah), is Arabic for patience, a quality which the humble Moslem must possess in abundance in order to resign himself to the hard lot in life which the Koran has foreordained. If you are visiting on a Thursday, you will see elderly Moslem women, some of them in purdah, their faces covered with a short black veil, coming to visit their dead. In the belief that the dead are able to hear all that is said to them, the women will make a full report of domestic events of the week.

As you scan the City Wall, you will note that there is no way of entering the Temple Mount from the east. During the Second Commonwealth there must have been at least one gate in this side of the wall, but all trace of it has been lost. About midway along the length of the wall you can make out a gate that has been closed for centuries. The **Golden Gate** was built by the Byzantines in the fourth century and remains Byzantine in form even though repairs and additions were made by Suleiman's architects. It is assumed that at the site of the Gate, or close to it, once stood the gateway that Jesus and other pilgrims throughout the Second Temple period used to enter the Temple Mount from the Mount of Olives. Today the Gate is sealed up and there is no way of entering the Temple Mount directly from outside the City. The Gate was probably closed for this very reason — to keep enemies from having direct access to the Temple Mount. But Jewish tradition holds that in the end of days the Messiah will enter Jerusalem on a white donkey through this gate, and that the Moslems, therefore, sealed it to prevent his coming. As a further precaution — so runs another legend — the Moslem cemetery was sited along the entire length of this wall, for the Messiah will stem from a priestly family and to this day Jewish law forbids a *cohen*, or priest, to approach the dead or even enter a burial place.

In the times of the Crusaders this gate was opened only once every year, on Palm Sunday, when pilgrims recreated the triumphal entry of Jesus into Jerusalem surrounded by followers shouting Hosanna and waving palm fronds which they cut from nearby trees. You will notice that, perhaps contrary to your expectations, there are only seven palm trees growing in this area. Botanists explain that palms do not thrive well under the severity of a Jerusalem winter. Perhaps overzealous pilgrims aided nature's destructive powers.

Continue walking along Jericho Road toward a sign that points into the valley on your right. Notice as you walk that the Kidron Valley is becoming deeper and more narrow. It begins north of the Old City Wall, continues along the entire eastern side of the Wall and ends a half-mile south of where you are now standing, cutting deeper and deeper into the earth's surface as it comes closer to its point of termination at the lowest spot in the Jerusalem area. The valley is relatively shallow at the portion that borders the Old City Wall, but it was not always thus. The Kidron Valley, associated with celestial revelations and the end of days, also served the most commonplace and everyday of city functions — a dumping ground for rubbish which has accumulated over the centuries, filling in the Kidron.

Now that you are stumbling down the rocky path leading into the Kidron Valley road, you can imagine what the entire stretch of the valley must have been like long ago, a canyon running the whole length of the city.

On the left of the road you will come upon the first of a row of four tombs which were built during the period of the Second Temple. The buildings of that greatest period of Jerusalem's development, with its palaces and mighty state buildings, its temples and its courts, lie buried deep below the surface of Jerusalem. Only these memorials to the dead have withstood winds, earthquakes, the storms of centuries, and conquerors who were thorough in their work of destruction. The architectural forms used in the memorials give us a clue to the forms used by builders during Second Temple Jerusalem. And the legends associated with the memorials evoke the strong ties that linked the Jews of the Second Temple with their ancestors who lived and wrote in the Biblical period.

All of these memorials have been carved out of the natural bed rock and are as strong as the mountain of which they were once a part. Indeed, the mountain continues to shelter each of them on three sides. The first and most impressive in the row of tombs is **Absalom's Memorial Pillar.** Absalom died about 11 centuries before the Common Era, but the mixture of decorative conventions on the "pillar" indicates that his memorial was constructed in the last part of the Second Commonwealth, some nine centuries after his death. The Jews of the Second Temple period never developed a style of architecture exclusively their own. The decorative motifs they used were taken from the styles established by the culture that happened to be the most prominent in the Middle East at the time of construction. As time went by and other cultural influences reached their zenith, the new trends were incorporated with the old and an eclectic style developed. Thus, the older the monument, the fewer its cultural influences. Because it was built later than were the three other tombs, Absalom's Pillar contains the largest assortment of architectural forms. The Egyptian influence came first and is represented by the heavy ridge or cornice that separates the square block carved out of the rock below the drums and spire which were added to the top. Beneath the cornice is a Doric frieze with a repetitive design of three stone bars and a circle. This was typical of the Greek influence during the days of the Hasmoneans. The Ionic pillars carved into the sides of the monolithic square are typical of the later Greek influence which spread throughout this part of the world with the ascendancy of Rome.

It wasn't called Absalom's Pillar until the days of the Crusaders, a jump of ten centuries from the time of the tomb's construction. Absalom was the best-loved of King David's many sons, most of whom wished to inherit their father's throne. "Now in all Israel there was no one so much to be praised for his beauty as Absalom; from the sole of his foot to the crown of his head there was no blemish in him. And when he cut the hair of his head (for at the end of every year he used to cut it, when it was heavy on him he cut it), he weighed the hair of his head, two hundred shekels by the king's weight." The story of his revolt against his father, the shamefulness of his death after it became clear he could not succeed, and the subsequent grief of his father as he cried, "O my son Absalom, my son, my son," is told in the *Book of Samuel II*, Chapters 15-18. Seat yourself as comfortably as possible on the lowest edge of Absalom's Pillar to read his story.

Walk behind Absalom's Pillar and to its left where you can see a pediment over the door of another ancient tomb, the **Tomb of Jehoshaphat**, again a reminder that only God judges in the end of days. This ancient sepulchre was uncovered in 1924. Its underground chambers are carved entirely out of the rock. It was hidden from view for such a long time probably because it served as a *genizah*, a place where wornout holy books are hidden. According to Jewish law holy books can never be willfully destroyed.

Stand at the opening and look up at the frieze. Since Jewish law prevented Jews of the Second Temple Period from carving human or animal figures, they covered the pediment of the tomb with floral motifs, particularly the lotus leaf, which repeats the theme of the lotus bud that tops Absalom's Pillar.

Continue walking into the valley. In a few steps, just before a patch of newly erected gravestones, a small dirt path on the left will lead you up to the rocks from which Absalom's Pillar was carved. It is interesting that all the graveyards round about are completely open to view as though they were as much a part of the city as its breathing sections. This is in contrast with cemeteries in western lands, which are closed off and hidden from view as though they posed an embarrassment to the living.

As you walk along the path keep your eyes on the rocks above. Suddenly you will see an artificial cave fronted by two carved pillars — the Tomb of the Sons of Hezir. Next to it is a monument similar to Absalom's Pillar, the Tomb of Zechariah. Both are earlier than Absalom's Pillar, for the Ionic or Roman influence does not appear at all. The Doric frieze on the Tomb of Hezir repeats the three stone bars you saw on the frieze of Absalom's Pillar. Similarly, the columns of the Tomb of Zechariah are Doric and the cornice and pyramid above are certainly Egyptian. Archaeologists, therefore, assume that these were built in the days of the Hasmoneans.

Hezir is the only historical name attached to these graves, and the individual members of the priestly family of Hezir are inscribed in ancient Hebrew on the facade of the grave. He was mentioned in the *Book of Nehemiah* and must have been a prominent gentleman for Nehemiah asked him to be one of the signers of the Declaration of Faith, a document that marked the return to Jerusalem at the end of the Babylonian exile. Nehemiah organized the community and assigned the various tasks needed to rebuild the nation. He also took measures to ensure that the returnees would not regress into the patterns of behavior which had brought upon them the First Exile. Nehemiah was a man who knew exactly what forms of self-discipline and community regimentation were required to effect this huge undertaking and did not confine his efforts to the verbal assaults favored by the prophets of the First Temple Days. They had failed to make the people of Israel obey the commandments of God and deal justly with their fellow men. Nehemiah's methods were tougher — and more successful. He "contended with them and cursed them and beat some of them and pulled out their hair." This is a good spot to stop and read the *Book of Nehemiah* from the eighth chapter to the thirteenth (skip the lists of names) where he describes the great joy of those who returned to Jerusalem and the enormous difficulties they faced, both joys and difficulties relived by the returnees of the twentieth century.

Over the centuries the Tomb of Zechariah has changed names frequently. It has been named after Joseph and Isaiah and Simeon, but the name of Zechariah remained permanently attached to this monument, possibly because the nation has never been able to make full atonement for the evil they did him. (Remember that the burial place you visited on the Mount of Olives was also assigned to Zechariah.)

Zechariah spoke out continuously and strongly against the deterioration of the society around him, not only to the people but to the king and his courtiers as well, telling them all the things they did not wish to hear. He saw clearly that the society was so weak and demoralized that it could not withstand any enemy attack. "Then the Spirit of God took possession of Zechariah the son of Jehoi'ada the priest; and he stood above the people and said to them, 'Thus says God, 'Why do you transgress the commandments of the Lord, so that you cannot prosper? Because you have forsaken the Lord, he has forsaken you.' But they conspired against him, and by command of the king they stoned him with stones in the court of the house of the Lord. Thus Joash the king did not remember the kindness which Jehoi'ada, Zechariah's father, had shown him, but killed his son." (*Chronicles II*, 24:20-22). On that day, so the wise men tell us, the king and Jerusalem committed not one but seven sins — they killed a priest, they killed a judge, they spilled innocent blood, they contaminated the Temple, and it was a Sabbath Day, and it was even the Day of Atonement. So horrible was this act — the murder of a prophet — that the wise men multiplied it by seven so that the conscience of the nation might never forget.

Walk around to the back of the Tomb of Zechariah. Notice with what primitive chisel strokes the ancient artisans wrested the monument from the face of the rock. Notice also that the upper portion of the rock face is darker than the lower, indicating that the bottom section of the tomb was hidden from view until a recent archaeological dig uncovered it once again.

An opening in the face of the rock leads directly into Hezir's Tomb. Take a short leap up to the opening and you will find yourself in an artificial cave. The marks of the Hasmonean stonecutter are clearly visible on the walls of the cave. Huge hatchets were used — a chisel couldn't possibly have done the job. When you get to the opening behind the two columns that you saw outside the tomb you will be standing in the entrance to a Second Temple burial chamber. An opening has been carved into the wall opposite the columns. Originally the opening was quite small. After a corpse was inserted into the burial rooms that lie beyond the small opening — large enough only for a small crawling undertaker — the entrance was sealed with a heavy stone to prevent grave robbers from entering. (Notice the slight groove that could accommodate such a stone.) During the Byzantine period, when these artificial caves served as living quarters for hermits, the openings were enlarged to man size.

Go through this opening and you will be in a second entrance hall. There are three openings in this hall. Enter the one directly in front of you to see exactly what a burial chamber of the Second Commonwealth Period looks like. There are three niches to accommodate three bodies. Actually, a corpse remained in the niche only until the flesh decomposed. Then the bones were placed in ossuaries, such as those you saw on the grounds of Dominus Flevit. The floor of a burial chamber can accommodate many ossuaries and thus a small cave can accommodate generations. It was a practical device in a mountainous country. This burial chamber is so typical of its genre that you need never enter another.

Back on the gravel path in front of the last tombs, look up at the buildings on the hill just ahead. They form the northern edge of the village of **Silwan**, which you will be skirting as you continue your walk into Kidron Valley. The buildings appear to be part of the mountain and indeed the cliffs themselves often form the first floors of the buildings. This form of architecture, while primitive, has been justly praised and Jerusalem architects are trying to recapture it in more modern ways, but they are getting only mixed notices.

Walk along the gravel path until it meets the paved Kidron Valley road. As you continue southward the walls of the Herodian enclosure of the Temple Mount will vanish from view and in its place on your right, you will see a huge slope with deep, jagged cuts. As you can tell from its charcoal-gray color, this slope is not a part of the mountains around you but is a man-made accretion of rubble which is constantly being eroded by rain and wind. As you continue walking, the color of the slope will change to the native warm tan. This is the slope of the **City of David**, rising on **Mount Ophel**. It is known that the hill was settled in pre-historic times. When first mentioned in the Bible, Jerusalem was occupied by the Jebusites, an ancient Canaanite tribe. It was a tiny enclave, but David saw it as his capital and the heart of the new nation. "And the King and his men went to Jerusalem against the Jebusites, the inhabitants of the land, who said to David, 'You will not come in here, but the blind and the lame will ward you off' — thinking, 'David cannot come in here'." The confidence of the Jebusites was inspired by the fact that their little village was surrounded on three sides by deep valleys and encircled by a thick wall of stone. The wall had to be built to a height considerably greater than the height of the Silwan mountain cliffs on your left; if the wall were lower it could not offer protection from enemy archers stationed there. The Jebusites could have found a higher, more defensible prominence in the area upon which to settle, but they were tied to the only source of natural water in the area, the **Spring of Gihon**, which lies at the base of Mount Ophel. In order to build the city wall to a height sufficient for safety, the Jebusites left the Spring of Gihon just outside the man-made boundaries of the city. And this was their undoing. Since the spring was outside the wall of the city and at a lower level than the wall, the primitive Jebusites had to dig a deep shaft on the ridge inside the city wall that descended beneath the wall until it reached the water source. Many scholars believe that David's army was able to enter and conquer the city via the Spring of Gihon and the shaft which led up into the City.

The exact location of the boundary walls of the City of David is a subject that has fascinated archaeologists for a century and the history of their surveys of this area fill volumes. New volumes will be written when the current dig -- described as **the** definitive dig -- comes to publishable conclusions.

When Nehemiah returned to Jerusalem after the Babylonian exile he also surveyed the boundaries of Jerusalem, but secretly, so as not to arouse the suspicions of the enemy — or, perhaps, not to encourage land speculation. The story of his midnight ride around the ruined walls is told in *Nehemiah*, Chapter 2: "Then I arose in the night, I and a few men with me; and I told no one what my God had put into my heart to do for Jerusalem. There was no beast with me but the beast on which I rode. I went out by night...and I inspected the walls of Jerusalem which were broken down and its gates which had been destroyed by fire ... but there was no place for the beast that was under me to pass. Then I went up ... by the valley and inspected the wall and turned back and entered by the Valley Gate, and so returned."

Stay on the right side of the road. The first building you come to is the **Silwan School**. Next to it is a kiosk and then comes the entrance to the **Spring of Gihon**. Gihon is a Hebrew word meaning "gusher," for the waters gush out at infrequent intervals, twice a day in the summer and five times a day in the winter. This phenomenon is common among springs found in similar geological strata, but in Jerusalem the gushing waters have given rise to innumerable legends. One of them, that Mary washed her infant's clothes here, accounts for the Gihon's synonym: the **Virgin's Fountain.**

Enter the Spring building and walk to a broad staircase descending between huge rock walls. A set of narrower stairs, slippery and wet, lead to an iron gate at the mouth of a rock cave which contains the spring. Now it is below ground, but during the days of the Jebusites, when the Kidron was much deeper than it is today, the spring bubbled at the surface.

Leading off to the left of the spring is **Hezekiah's Tunnel**, a dark path under the ground which was hewn out of the hard rock 3,000 years ago. In the year 700 B.C. Hezekiah, a king of Judah, remembering the history of his people on this hill, and fearing that an enemy may be able to enter the city through the spring as David did, decided to bring the waters of the Gihon into the city and store them in the Pool of Shiloah to ensure a steady supply of water during times of siege and war, as well as of peace. He sealed the opening to the spring so that it could not be used as a means of entering the city itself. "Sennacherib king of Assyria came and invaded Judah and encamped against the fortified cities, thinking to win them for himself. And when Hezekiah saw that Sennacherib had come and intended to fight against Jerusalem, he planned with his officers and high mighty men to stop the water of the springs that were outside the city, and they helped him... Hezekiah closed the upper outlet of the waters of Gihon and directed them down to the west side of the city of David." (*Chronicles II*, 32).

It is possible to walk through the entire tunnel — 600 yards in length — and come out at the southwestern edge of the City of David. The water never rises above thigh level, so all you have to do is strip to your bathing suit and wade in. (If you haven't brought your bathing suit just keep reading until you get to the section with further instructions for land-bound visitors.) Don't attempt this part of the walk without a flashlight. As you walk through the rushing waters notice that the tunnel swerves in and out along its entire length, as though the engineers were not quite sure which direction to follow in order to end up at the pool. It appears as though they were correcting their mistakes as they went along. Perhaps they were searching for soft veins in the rock. Another team of diggers was moving from the Pool at the southern end of the tunnel in an effort to meet the diggers moving in the direction you are now walking. That the two teams did in fact meet, without any instruments to enable them to judge their distance from one another, is indeed a "genuine miracle." The moment of that astonishing meeting was recorded by an anonymous digger with a historical bent. He carved the following inscription on the wall of the tunnel: "This is the boring through. This is the story of the boring through. Whilst the miners lifted the pick each toward his fellow and while three cubits yet remained to be bored through, there was heard the voice of a man calling to his fellow, for there was a split in the rock on the right hand and on the left hand, and on the day of the boring through the miners struck each in the direction of his fellow, pick against pick, and the water started flowing from the source to the pool, 1200 cubits, and 100 cubits was the height of the rock above the heads of the miners."

This **Shiloah Inscription** was discovered in 1880 by two adventurous Jewish boys who wanted to see for themselves the mysterious ghosts who were said to inhabit the tunnel. They lost their matches and were forced to walk in the dark, feeling their way over the rough stone, until their fingertips touched the carved inscription. (Do not inquire how they could have known it was an inscription without any light, for the story is perfect in itself, as all such stories are.) The inscription was authenticated by a number of famous Jerusalem archaeologists who labored together over the ancient Hebrew text until they had deciphered it to their satisfaction. It is said that a greedy Greek antiquities dealer stole into the tunnel in the dead of night and chiseled the inscription out of its bed of rock, with a view to selling it for a high fee. However, he was apprehended by the Turkish police who punished him severely, and shipped the inscription to the Museum in Istanbul, where it can be seen today. As you walk through the waters notice the niches carved in the rock above. Scholars assume that these provided resting places for the torches of the workmen.

If you prefer your adventures dry, you can reach the **Pool of Shiloah** from above ground, where the path leading from the Gihon to the Pool is only 400 yards in length. (If you have had enough, walk across the road and take the Arab bus back to the East Jerusalem Central Bus Station opposite Damascus Gate — another form of dry adventure.)

But if you do decide to continue on to the pool you must return to the road bordering the village of **Silwan**, rising to your left along the whole length of the slope opposite the City of David. In the center of the lowest level of Silwan is a huge rock outcropping which is assumed to be the **Stone of Zohelet**, mentioned in the biblical story of David's son Adonijah's attempt to gain the throne just before his father's death. "Now Adonijah the son of Haggith exalted himself, saying, 'I will

The Waters of Rogel and the Well as once it was

be king'; and he prepared for himself chariots and horsemen... Adonijah sacrificed sheep, oxen and fatlings by the Stone of Zohelet, which is beside Ein Rogel (the termination of today's walk), and he invited all his brothers, the king's sons." But Bathsheba, the mother of Solomon, had been promised the throne for her son and she went to David as he lay dying to remind him of his pledge. Knowing that the Stone of Zohelet where Adonijah and his followers were camped, was in full view of the Gihon spring (remember that in those days the Gihon was above ground), King David instructed the priest Zadok to "Take with you the servants of your lord, and cause Solomon my son to rise on my own mule, and bring him down to Gihon... and there anoint him king over Israel; then blow the trumpet, and say, 'Long live King Solomon'." It is with this story that the *First Book of Kings* opens.

Now is the time to stop for an antiquities browse in the little shop on the right side of the road. Even if you don't find something you would like or can afford to buy, have a cold drink and an amiable chat with the owners.

At the southern end of the City of David you will find a path on your right that leads to a small mosque. In front of it is the **Pool of Shiloah.** Notice that in the water itself there are a number of white and red remnants of marble pillars, all that remains of a church that stood here in the fifth century to commemorate Jesus' opening the eyes of the blind with the waters of the pool.

Retrace your steps to the road and follow the valley to a thick stand of fig trees on your left that marks the meeting place of the Kidron, the Hinnom and the Tyropoeon Valleys. The road curves around this heavily wooded place. Up ahead you will see a cliff of jagged black rocks climbing up to a silver-colored dome that marks the **Monastery of Acel Dama,** the potter's field purchased with Judas Iscariot's thirty pieces of silver.

Now the road forks; take the left tine and you will see a sign pointing toward **Bir Ayub,** known also as the **Waters of Rogel.** Follow the arrow to a clearing among the fig trees in the center of which there is an ancient well. When it overflows during a year of bountiful rainfall there is joy among the workers of the field. This is an idyllic spot; rest here and observe Arab village life. Buy a cold drink at the little kiosk and watch the Arab women from the village of Silwan tending their fig trees in the same spot where the Garden of the Kings once stood. Then walk back to the road where an Arab bus will take you to the Damascus Gate bus station. You've had a busy day.

THE SECOND WALK

FROM REMEZ SQUARE TO MOUNT ZION

The core of this walk is Mount Zion, one among the many mountains upon which Jerusalem is built. It is not a separate entity but only the last segment of a chain of hills that begins north of the Old City Wall, enters the Old City and extends along its entire western side. Because it is physically so intimately related to the Old City, Mount Zion's exclusion from the circuit of the Wall comes as a surprise. Mount Zion was certainly inside the Wall during the days of the Second Temple. Some say it was included within the Wall even in the days of the First Temple, some twenty-five centuries ago. When the architects hired by Sultan Suleiman to reconstruct the Wall in 1546 failed to include Mount Zion, they were summarily beheaded. So the legend goes. In fact, Zion and Jerusalem have always been inseparable, as a word and as a concept, if not as one specific place.

This walk begins at the **Central Railroad Station.** From the center of town, Bus Nos. 6 or 7 will let you off just in front of the stationhouse. It was constructed in 1892 by the Turks to adorn the first railroad line in the Middle East, pre-dating even the famed Orient Express. Then, the railway was a narrow track providing infrequent and casual service between Jerusalem and Jaffa on the coast. Enlarged and brought up to relatively modern service standards it is now part of a system that

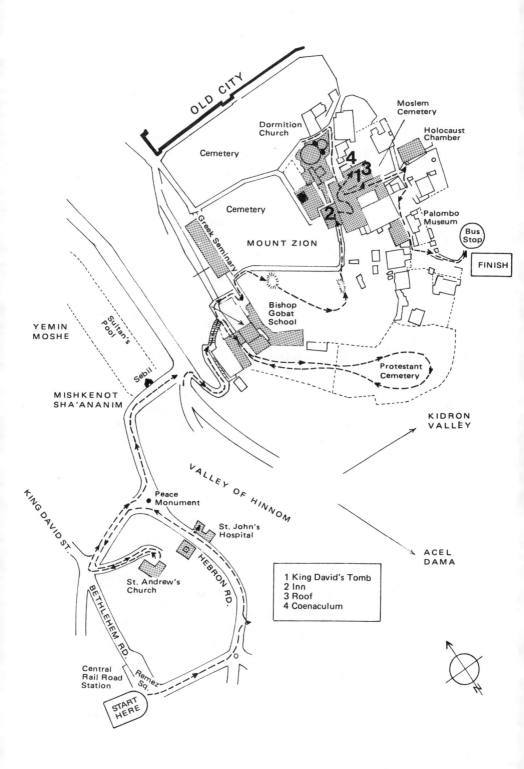

OLD CITY

Moslem Cemetery

Holocaust Chamber

Dormition Church

Cemetery

4
7 **3**

2

Cemetery

Palombo Museum

Greek Seminary

MOUNT ZION

Bus Stop

FINISH

YEMIN MOSHE

Sultan's Pool

Bishop Gobat School

Sebil

MISHKENOT SHA'ANANIM

Protestant Cemetery

KIDRON VALLEY

VALLEY OF HINNOM

KING DAVID ST.

Peace Monument

St. John's Hospital

ACEL DAMA

BETHLEHEM RD.

HEBRON RD.

St. Andrew's Church

1 King David's Tomb
2 Inn
3 Roof
4 Coenaculum

Central Rail Road Station

Remez Sq.

START HERE

N

links Jerusalem to a network of cities, among them, Haifa, Beersheba, Dimona and, under normal circumstances, even the Gaza Strip.

Cross **Remez Square** on the painted white lines. (Pedestrians always have the right of way at such crossings.) The exposed rock strata on this side of the street borders a large empty space which served as the campsite for Pompey's army in 63 B.C. and for the British Forces Indian Regiment in World War I. Both came to conquer, and succeeded.

Walk down the street toward the traffic lights until it forks into four separate streets. Take the one on your left, **Hebron Road**. As you make the turn into this street, you will see a lovely view of Jerusalem. In the center of the panorama is **Mount Zion**, distinguished by the cone-shaped metal roof and bell tower of the **Dormition Church**. Cross to the other side of the street for a better view of the area south of Mount Zion.

About midway down the block, just past a rise in the stone wall bordering the road, is a good place from which to look into the **Valley of Hinnom**. At this location you can see how the valley turns eastward to form the southern boundary of the Old City. The valley continues in an easterly line until it meets the Kidron Valley at the lowest point in the Jerusalem network of valleys. (It might be helpful to conceive of these two valleys, the Hinnom on the west and south of the Old City, the Kidron on the east, as a geometrical configuration. They form a huge triangle, with the square of the Old City lying within the angle. This large triangle is bisected into two smaller triangles by the Tyropoeon Valley, which runs through the Old City and meets the angle formed by the Kidron and the Hinnom.) You can see the point where the three valleys meet in a triangle of dense vegetation dipping down below the surrounding mountains. Above this green triangle and farther out on the eastern horizon is another large patch of dense greenery surrounded entirely by a stone wall. From this distance it looks like a huge pot for a gigantic plant. It is the **Hill of Scandal**, where King Solomon scandalized his subjects by having altars built to the numerous idols worshipped by his cosmopolitan wives.

Continue down the road a few more paces till you come to a low, yellow-stoned building. It was once **St. John's Ophthalmic Hospital**, built by the Knights of St. John in 1912, to help combat the eye diseases then so prevalent in this part of the world. The facade of the building is lined with stone tablets bearing coats of arms. Notice that even those with the most traditionally English motifs include a rigid, stylized hand, the middle-eastern symbol for good luck. The bars on the windows form Maltese crosses, the heraldic symbol of the Order of St. John. The yellow building blocks are made of soft limestone which, though lovely, is not sufficiently weather-resistant. The pockmarks in the walls were not caused by bullets, as in other places you will see, but rather by the natural elements. The building is composed of a series of wings, each with a separate entrance. Enter the very last entrance, and ask someone to show you the rusty crank. Be insistent, for the crank and its iron cable is a historical monument and must be left open to public view. Three days after the declaration of the State, the Israeli army captured Mount Zion. Then, a group of construction men met in this building to devise a way of bridging the valley between West Jerusalem and Mount Zion so that the defenders of the hill could be provided with supplies and re-enforcements. The Legionnaires occupied the ramparts of the Old City Wall and could easily pick off anyone attempting to come to the aid of those on Mount Zion. The construction workers decided on an iron cable which could be stretched taut from St. John's to the Gobat Institute on Mount Zion. Men and supplies swung across only at night; the cable was lowered to lie slack on the valley floor during the day.

Cross the road outside of St. John's and enter the **Jerusalem House of Quality**, another wing of the former hospital. It has been renovated recently to provide work- and display-space for artisans. Notice that the coats of arms you saw across the street have been retained in the inner courtyard of the renovated building. The salesrooms are open daily. It's a lovely place to browse leisurely. But don't miss the workshops on the second floor where you can see how the art objects are made.

When you leave the House of Quality turn left and follow the road which will take you to **St. Andrew's Church**, the white-domed, yellow-stoned (again, the porous limestone) building on your left. The church was built in 1927 to honor the men of Scotland who had died in the conquest of Jerusalem during World War I. The building is an excellent example of a British adaptation of European and middle-eastern architectural forms. Those who viewed England solely as a colonial power saw its architectural forms, too, as an outgrowth of imperialism.

The major portion of the building is a hospice for pilgrims who wish to enjoy the spectacular view of Jerusalem in tranquility. The church itself can be entered from a side staircase, but only with the assistance of a staff member. The interior was planned with great care, from the

Italian-glass windows to the fine Florentine wrought-iron gate. The marble in the altar was imported from Scotland. A plaque in the floor recounts the legend of Robert Bruce, the king who united the independent Scots tribes into one nation by appealing to them to join the Crusades. He asked that his heart be buried in Jerusalem, close to the Holy Grave of Jesus. The messenger bearing his heart met with misadventures on the dangerous route to Jerusalem and had to return to Scotland. King Bruce's body is buried in one church in Scotland, his heart in another, but his devotion to Jerusalem is recorded here.

Take the church road bearing left to the busy intersection of **Bethlehem Road, Hebron Road,** and **King David Street.** The sign opposite reads "Mount Zion 500 meters." Turn to your right. In front of you is a monument by a well-known contemporary sculptor, Tamarkin. It was commissioned by Abie Natan, the Israeli who achieved fame by his use of unconventional methods of promoting peace with Egypt. The **Peace Monument** was erected on the edge of "no-man's land" just a few months before the Six-Day War. The Hebrew and Arabic inscriptions are from Isaiah: "And they shall beat their swords into ploughshares, their spears into pruning hooks; nation shall not lift sword against nation; neither shall they learn war any more." The platform surrounding the monument is an excellent observation point from which to see the Valley of Hinnom as it turns toward the east. Mount Zion as an integral part of the Old City can also be most easily understood from this observation point.

Keep walking on **Hebron Road**, a route known to have been in use since the Days of the Patriarchs. This is a busy street, so be sure to get over to the side of the road that has a sidewalk. The area below on your right is said to be the most notorious spot in the Valley of Hinnom. Here, in the Days of the Kings, Jews worshipped the idol Moloch, a most hideous form of idolatry that demanded the sacrifice of young children. From this practice, in this place, came the word for "hell" — *Gehenna* — the Greek form of *Gai Hinnom*, or Valley of Hinnom.

Rashi, the eleventh-century commentator on the Bible, describes Moloch as a bronze god with arms outstretched. The parents themselves were required to place the child on the burning arms of the god and stand by calmly to watch. If they expressed any emotion the sacrifice was declared "unclean." The priests of the idol played loudly on drums (*tupim*) to drown out the shrieks of the children; thus the name **Tofet** by which this place is also known. At least two of the kings of Judah

The Valley of Hinnom,
with ancient burial caves on the left.
Hopefully, the caves are not used
as dwellings today.

sacrificed their sons to Moloch. The *Book of Chronicles* tells that King
Ahaz, who ruled in the seventh century B.C., and King Manasseh, who
ruled 30 years later, burned their sons in the Valley of Hinnom.

The land in the foreground descends toward the right. Nearby is a
small plateau bisected by a number of sand paths. Among the paths you
can make out a series of burial caves used in the days of the Second

Temple. During that period caves carved out of natural rocks were used
for burial; graves dug into the ground are a later invention. These particular burial caves are mentioned in the New Testament. After Judas
Iscariot received his payment from the priests for betraying Jesus he
was stricken with remorse and returned the thirty pieces of silver. The
priests used the blood money to purchase a burial field for paupers and
called it **Acel Dama,** or Field of Blood. (You passed the monastery
marking the site on your First Walk.) Greek inscriptions found on the
caves indicate that they provided permanent homes for monks of the
Byzantine period.

Keep on **Hebron Road** as it bears right. This part of the road is
actually a dam, known to have originated in the Herodian period. It was
reconstructed and renovated in various periods of history to keep the
rain water collecting in the Valley of Hinnom from running off on its
natural course into the Dead Sea. The dam provides the base for a particularly handsome **sebil** built by Sultan Suleiman which, unfortunately,
no longer provides water, as it did in the 1500's, for the thirsty pilgrim
to Mount Zion. During the 1948 War of Independence a tunnel was dug
from the nearby settlement of **Yemin Moshe** to Mount Zion to provide
an escape route for wounded soldiers. It was, of course, impossible to
use the road itself for this purpose. The tunnel runs directly beneath
the stone wall bordering the dam.

Hebron Road intersects with **Jerusalem Brigade Road** at the base
of Mount Zion. There are two roads immediately on your right, one
descending, one ascending. Take the latter. On your left, as you climb
this road, there are a series of partially roofed holes, the remains of the
tunnel linking Mount Zion and Yemin Moshe.

You are now "going up to Zion," the aim of pilgrims to Jerusalem
for centuries. During the days of the First and Second Temples pilgrims
came to Jerusalem on three holidays, Passover, Shavuot and Succot, to
fulfill the Biblical commandment: "Three times a year all your males
shall appear before the Lord your God at the place which he will
choose: at the feast of unleavened bread, at the feast of weeks and at
the feast of booths." After the destruction of the Second Temple in
70 A.D., Jews, when permitted to by the various governors of Jerusalem
through the succeeding centuries, came to the Western Wall, all that
remained of the Temple grounds, to mourn the destruction and pray
for the Return to Zion. For the twenty-year period between the War of
Independence and the Six-Day War, even that was not possible. So

Mount Zion, the closest accessible point to the Temple Mount, became the focus of pilgrimages to Jerusalem.

As you climb up the mountain look down into the Valley of Hinnom and to the hill beyond. That tall, handsome domed building with the Union Jack flying nearby is the St. Andrew's Church you have just visited. The long, low-slung, red-roofed building on the hill on your right is **Mishkenot Sha'ananim,** the first settlement to be built by Jews outside the Wall of the Old City. Its newly cleaned stones form a bold line on the crest of the hill. To visualize how lonely it must have looked when it was built in 1860, you will have to erase mentally all surrounding development (the gardens especially) and reconstruct in your mind's eye the wall that began at the point where you can still see the remains of a stone gateway, and that encircled the building on all sides.

The road twists back on itself as you climb higher and opens up views on places you will visit on the next walks in this book — the arcade of arches on the Pontifical Biblical Institute, the Windmill above Mishkenot Sha'ananim, the tower of the Y.M.C.A. and the King David Hotel.

At one point, the road becomes a staircase. At the top of the stairs and on your right is the **Bishop Gobat School and Institute,** a Protestant seminary and research center. The stone wall beside the entrance to the school contains a number of carved blocks from the Herodian period. More of them can be found inside the entrance to the school. Why are these chiseled rocks significant? Besides giving us incontestable evidence that Mount Zion was included within the walls of Jerusalem as far back as the days of the Second Temple, the discovery of the rocks heralded the beginning of a period of intensive archaeological exploration in Jerusalem. For one hundred years Jerusalem has been the magnet for teams of scholars from many lands who have attempted to uncover and reconstruct Jerusalem's past. The digs of those early explorers uncovered remnants of ancient walls. From the stones, their form and placement, much has been learned about the shape of Jerusalem and the style of living of its inhabitants during long-known but little-understood periods of history. The early archaeologists used meager equipment and old-fashioned techniques, the later ones a more scientific approach. In 1874 Henry Maudsley began to dig on Mount Zion and uncovered a long wall dating from the days of the Second Temple, a system of waterworks and the bed rock foundations of a tower. Carrying on his work, the English team of Bliss and Dickey uncovered a wall one kilometer in length, with five towers, and a paved road leading into the city. Unfortunately, most of what they uncovered during a three-year expedition, beginning in 1894, had to be reburied, but they left careful maps and a lengthy report — an extremely interesting document that records not only their findings but the everyday difficulties they encountered with their native staff of diggers and with the owners of the properties through which they had to dig in order to follow the course of the wall.

The Bishop Gobat Institute itself is a complex structure with many wings and elements that were tacked on as needs changed. The unifying element is the bed rock upon which many of its sections were built. This bed rock, which can be clearly seen in the entrance and on the second floor of the Ecumenical Institute, was formerly a sharp cliff, or escarpment, which was carved out of natural rock and which defined the defensive line of the ancient walls.

You should follow the instructions posted on the front door of the Institute. Don't be put off by the locked gate; this is a most friendly place. The Protestant cemetery which lies at the back of the Institute gardens is interesting from many aspects. Many of the gravestones are inscribed with quotations in Hebrew. The German soldiers who were allies of the Turks in World War I lie buried beside the British soldiers who fought against them. The graves of British soldiers who were killed in the Resistance are here, including those who died in the bombing of the King David Hotel. Conrad Schick and Sir Petrie, two pioneers of Jerusalem exploration, are also buried in this cemetery. Many of the names carved into the headstones are obviously the Jewish names of converts to Christianity.

The views of the city from the edges of the cemetery are extraordinary and not to be missed.

When you leave the Bishop Gobat Institute walk straight ahead. A series of signs will point the way to **King David's Tomb**. The first building you come to on your way is shared by Orthodox Jews who manage the lower floor and Greek Orthodox seminarians who study on the second floor.

The yellow signs will lead you through a large open space containing four pits. These are archaeological digs. The first three uncovered water pits assumed to have been used by dyers to tint fabrics. It is known that this was an industrial area during the Roman and Byzantine periods, and cloth-dyeing was for centuries a major industry in

The complex housing the Tomb of David and the Coenaculum:
a view uncluttered by 20th century development

Jerusalem. The fourth dig appears to have been granted unwarranted significance by the modern concrete structure built around it.

A stone pavement will lead you into the main arcade of the building housing King David's Tomb. It is a dark room, almost a cave, supported by huge primitive-looking pillars. You are standing in an inn built at the end of the fourteenth century. There are rings on the walls to keep the horses in place; the travelers themselves were put up on the second floor. It should not be surprising to find that someone in the 1300's thought that King David's Tomb was a proper site for a hotel. The entire site of the Tomb is complex, providing within a relatively small area space to express a wide range of beliefs and functions quite unrelated to King David. In fact, scholarly evidence strongly suggests that King David could not have been buried on Mount Zion. It is often assumed that the burial chamber purported to be his was actually built for an anonymous Crusader.

The Crusaders themselves followed a tradition established earlier by the Byzantines that here, on an ancient burial site, Jesus and his disciples shared the Last Supper. The Crusaders built the Coenaculum within this complex of buildings to memorialize the event. The Moslems used the site to erect a number of mosques, for they hold King David in reverence as a prophet. Thus, King David's Tomb is holy to all three religions whose past is intimately linked with Jerusalem.

The darkened arcade opens onto an interior courtyard. Tacked onto a wall on your left is a narrow staircase that rises to the roof of the building. On the first landing there are three exquisite Crusader windows that you will see once again when you enter the Coenaculum.

The dome and minaret on the roof are part of the mosque within the building. Between 1948 and 1967 when Jews could not enter the Old City, this rooftop was the closest accessible place to the Western Wall where they could pray. The **Dormition Tower**, on your left as you look out over the Old City, was badly damaged in the 1948 Battle for Jerusalem and was only recently repaired.

Look over the side of the roof at the back of the dome into the small cemetery below. It belongs to the Dejanis, a family that was entrusted by the Turks with the hereditary task of guarding the Tomb. This family had the duty, as did all families entrusted with the care of specific holy places, to enforce the government's decisions as to who could and who could not visit the site. At various periods in the history of this trusteeship the family would not permit Jews to enter the Tomb, nor Christians the Coenaculum. The dome on the roof stands immediately above both the Coenaculum on the second floor and the Tomb on the first floor.

Walk up the narrow staircase in the minaret. There is a perfect 360-degree angle view of the City from the top.

Return to the staircase. When you reach the bottom make a U-turn to the right, walk through the facing wrought-iron gate and turn left into one of the anterooms of King David's Tomb. The Jewish tradition that King David is buried here was first mentioned by Benjamin of Tudela, the twelfth-century pilgrim who carefully recorded all of his impressions of Jerusalem. He recounts the building of a church on Mount Zion in 1158. In the course of digging the foundations, workers uncovered a stone-covered burial cave. "One of them said to his mate, 'Let us go and see if there is any money in it.' So they proceeded through the cave till they reached a great palace...A sudden gust of wind came from the mouth of the cave...crying with the voice of man: 'Rise and go hence, for God doth not desire to show it to man.'" The flashes of lightning and thunder that accompanied the voice forced the men to come to the conclusion that this was the long-sought-after tomb of David. Al-Mukaddasi, a famous Moslem historian, records this as the burial place of David even earlier, in the tenth century. Although there have been scholarly demurrers to this tradition, centuries of pilgrims have themselves made the site holy.

As you approach the tomb you will notice families taking meals out of lunch baskets. This is a common practice among Oriental Jews who come to the graves of the forefathers and sages to mourn in a keening wail for a full day or more.

In the small anteroom to the tomb there is a *mihrab* set into the wall on the right of the entrance wall. This decoration is found in all mosques. It points the way to Mecca, the direction toward which the devout Moslem must face when saying his prayers. In the narrow room of the tomb a depression was found in the wall behind the grave. Depressions shaped like this suggest three possibilities to archaeologists: a *mihrab*, an apse from a Christian church, or the front altar of a Jewish synagogue. Since the depression does not point south toward Mecca it cannot be a *mihrab*; since it does not mark the east wall it cannot be an apse; but it does point north toward the Temple Mount, and Jews, no matter where they pray in the world, must face in the direction of the Second Temple site. Scholars, therefore, believe that this room was once also a synagogue, possibly one of the early ones built in Jerusalem. Although synagogues were built even in the days of the Second Temple, their exact location is unknown. However, it is recorded that after the destruction of the Second Temple in 70 A.D. the Romans forbade Jews from entering the walled city. They were thus forced to build a number of synagogues on Mount Zion.

The tomb you see is really the headstone of a burial chamber, in the form used by the Crusaders, covered by a synagogue altar cover. Modern pilgrims often hire the services of a pious man to say prayers beside the grave of King David for their own dead.

Leave the tomb and walk back to the corridor in front of the wrought-iron gate. Turn right, walk through another iron gate and down a set of semicircular stairs. The wall of the building on your right contains a dramatic example of the use of the remains of one structure to build another. The small pillars once framed an opening into one of the courtyards of this building. This structure is so complex because the function of the building changed frequently as time went on. A succession of occupants tacked new elements onto the old to make the building continue its usefulness for still another century. The process continues today as the building's current occupants make their own changes and additions.

Enter the first opening on your right. The well-worn staircase on your left leads up to the Coenaculum, the Latin word for dining hall. Two of the most significant events recorded in the New Testament are said to have taken place here: the last Passover feast shared by Jesus and his disciples, which gave rise to the sacrament of the bread and the wine; and the Pentecost Assembly. In the *Gospel According to Mark* the story of the Last Supper is told thus: "And on the first day of Unleavened Bread, when they sacrificed the passover lamb, his disciples said to him, 'Where will you have us go and prepare for you to eat the passover?' and he sent two of his disciples, and said to them, 'Go into the city, and a man carrying a jar of water will meet you: follow him, and wherever he enters, say to the householder, "The Teacher says, Where is my guest room, where I am to eat the passover with my disciples?" And he will show you a large upper room furnished and ready; there prepare for us.'" The Gospel tells what occurred during that meal: "And as they were eating, he took bread, and blessed and broke it, and gave it to them, and said, 'Take; this is my body.' And he took a cup and when he had given thanks he gave it to them, and they all drank of it. And he said to them, 'This is my blood of the covenant, which is poured out for many.'"

Pentecost, the Christian festival, is observed seven weeks after the Passover feast, as is the Jewish holiday of Shavuot. *The Acts of the Apostles* describes how, on that day, the disciples once again "went up to the upper room," to pray. "And suddenly a sound came from heaven like the rush of a might wind...And there appeared to them tongues as of fire, distributed and resting on each one of them. And they were all filled with the Holy Spirit and began to speak in other tongues...and they were bewildered, because each one heard them speaking in his own language." In other words, it was the presence of the Holy Spirit that enabled them to speak and understand languages that they did not know. Peter, trying to explain the meaning behind the event, quotes from the prophet Joel: "I will pour out my Spirit upon all flesh, and your sons and your daughters shall prophesy, and your

young men shall see visions, and your old men shall dream dreams."
In the course of his sermon on the Pentecost, Peter says, "Brethren, I
may say to you confidently of the patriarch David that he both died
and was buried, and his tomb is with us to this day." It is probably
because of this reference that the Pentecost Assembly was believed to
have been on the "upper floor" of King David's Tomb.

Many Christian groups make a pilgrimage to the Coenaculum on the
Pentecost, just at the time when Jews are making their annual Shavuot
pilgrimage to the Temple Mount.

The history of the Coenaculum shifts between destruction and
renovation, expulsion and return. In 390 A.D. the Byzantines erected a
huge basilica named Hagia Zion, the Mother of Churches, to preserve
both the site of the Last Supper and the place where Mary, the mother
of Jesus, closed her eyes for the last time. (These two events are now
memorialized by two separate structures, the first by the Coenaculum,
the second by the Dormition Church.) Hagia Zion was burned to its
foundations by the Persians in 614 A.D., was rebuilt some twenty years
later and remained in place until 966 when the Moslems destroyed it
again. Remains of these earlier structures have been found in the course
of archaeological explorations of the site. The later history of the
Coenaculum can be found in the room itself. The room is of classical
Crusader construction. Note the pillar to the right of the entrance that
still bears the Crusader shield symbol. The Crusaders renewed the destroyed memorial to the Last Supper when they came to Jerusalem "to
rescue the holy places from the hands of the infidel."

When the Moslems forced the retreat of the Crusaders from Jerusalem they converted many Christian holy places into mosques. The
Coenaculum was spared until 1552, at which time Christians were
barred from entering the Coenaculum and the room was turned into a
mosque. A *mihrab* stands on the Coenaculum's right wall, pointing the
way to Mecca and hiding one of the three Crusader windows cut into
the wall of the building which you saw as you climbed to its top.

For centuries Jews were forbidden to enter the Tomb and
Christians to enter the Coenaculum. Not until 1948, when Mount Zion
became a part of the new State of Israel, were Christians and Jews free
to enter. However, there is no direct connection between the Christian
and Jewish parts of the building (the Coenaculum and King David's
Tomb) although it would not be difficult to effect such a connection.
Thus, Christian pilgrims and Jewish pilgrims need never meet and

The Mount of Olives as seen from Mount Zion, both in their former pristine states

mingle when they visit their common holy place.

Descend the staircase. Turn right on the stone pavement outside the Coenaculum and pay a visit to the **Dormition Church.** The road which follows the outline of the building runs between two high stone walls and veers to the left. Just past the entrance to the church there are two cemeteries closed off by iron gates. One of them is decorated with skulls and crossbones, the symbol of Golgotha, or Calvary, where Jesus died, a place of suffering and sacrifice. On the top of the iron gate are the Greek letters "t" and "p" which stand for *taphos*, or holy grave.

Enter the Dormition Church, a relatively new structure built in 1910 by the German Order of the Benedictines on part of the earlier Hagia Zion. The mosaic floor traces the prophetic tradition in a series of widening circles. The inner circle contains the symbol of the Trinity with the word holy repeated three times in Greek; the next circle, the four major prophets; the names of the twelve lesser prophets in the next circle; and the twelve Apostles in the next. The signs of the Zodiac in the final circle are surrounded by a Latin quotation from the *Book of Proverbs* which begins, "Ages ago I was created, at the first, before the beginning of the earth."

Each of the mosaics in the glowing side altars was designed by a different artist. The names of the various workshops in Germany that executed the designs are included in the mosaics. The mosaic in the upper part of the apse pictures Mary and Jesus and below is inscribed the line from Isaiah: "Behold a virgin shall conceive and bear a son and his name shall be called Emmanuel."

A staircase leads down into the cellar where there is an effigy of Mary on a sarcophagus bathed in dramatic light. The overpowering smell of burning wax is a common feature of holy places.

When you leave through the Dormition's iron gate turn right on the stone pavement to return to the building containing the Tomb of David. Walk past the entrance to the Tomb, and turn left into a corridor leading into a dark chamber. Candles will be burning in the ledges built onto the pillars of the chamber. The whole room is black with the carbon of countless candles burned here to the memory of King David.

Across the road immediately outside the exit from this room, is the **Martef Hasho'ah**, the Holocaust Chamber. The Hebrew inscription at the entrance reads: "The blood of your brothers cries out." White stone tablets line the walls of the chambers, each recording the name of another town in Europe that was destroyed by the Nazis during the Second World War. In one chamber you will see a row of blue and white earthenware goblets containing the ashes found in concentration camps throughout Europe and brought here for reburial.

When you leave the Holocaust Chamber, turn left and walk into the **Palombo Museum** across the road. Here you will see the original work of the sculptor whose excellence is attested to by the many artists who have copied his style. Ask the museum guide to light the torches Palombo designed as an example of the kind of lighting he thought should be provided at holy places. Particularly effective is the one designed for the nighttime ceremony at Modi'in during which new recruits of the Armoured Corps pledge themselves to the nation.

Turn right outside the museum and follow the curving road. The Number 1 bus stop and the end of the walk is nearby.

THE THIRD WALK

FROM WINGATE SQUARE THROUGH THE GERMAN COLONY

This walk begins at the focal point of the most elegant neighborhood in Jerusalem, where the best efforts of British, Arab, and Jewish architects and townplanners can be viewed. As you wander from this neighborhood into the equally lovely but entirely different German Colony you will get a chance to see one new theater and an old-new one, two museums, the President's residence, and churches built by people from widely separated and distant lands that all look quite at home on the same Jerusalem hill. You will end the walk in Jerusalem's newest garden, a stage set from which to view the southwestern part of the Old City Walls. You might try this walk on Saturday when both museums are open. The theater will be closed but you must visit it during performance time, in any event.

Bus No. 15, coming from the center of town, will let you off on a wide thoroughfare, **Jabotinsky Street.** (Ask the driver to let you off at the Sokolov Street intersection.) Up ahead is **Wingate Square,** easily distinguished by the round island at its center. The square is often referred to by local residents as Salome Square, in honor of the wealthy Arab who purchased all the four bordering lots. He wanted to make sure that all the facing buildings would be of uniform high quality and appropriate in scale and style to the square itself and to one another.

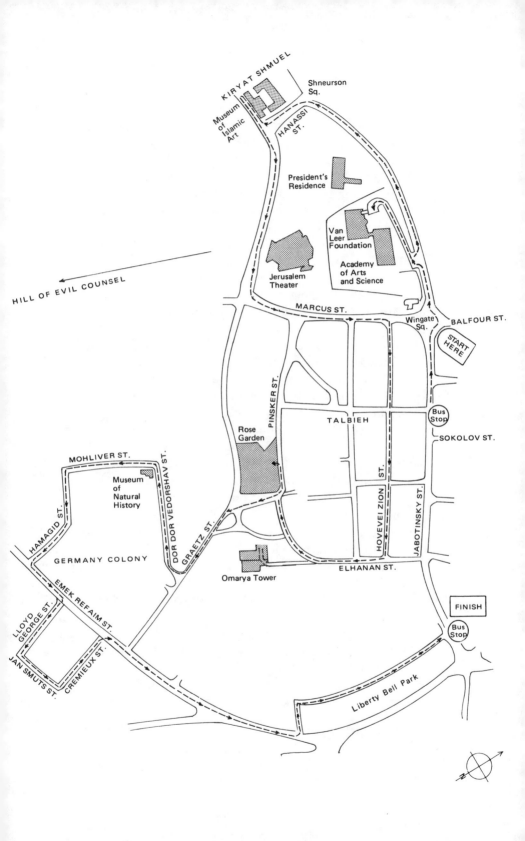

KIRYAT SHMUEL

Shneurson Sq.

Museum of Islamic Art

HANASSI ST.

President's Residence

Van Leer Foundation

Academy of Arts and Science

Jerusalem Theater

HILL OF EVIL COUNSEL

MARCUS ST.

Wingate Sq.

BALFOUR ST.

START HERE

PINSKER ST.

TALBIEH

Bus Stop

SOKOLOV ST.

Rose Garden

MOHLIVER ST.

DOR DOR VEDORSHAV ST.

Museum of Natural History

HAMAGID ST.

GRAETZ ST.

HOVEVEI ZION ST.

JABOTINSKY ST.

GERMANY COLONY

EMEK REFAIM ST.

Omarya Tower

ELHANAN ST.

LLOYD GEORGE ST.

JAN SMUTS ST.

CREMIEUX ST.

FINISH

Bus Stop

Liberty Bell Park

Two other streets enter this square, **Marcus** and **Balfour.** Their tree-lined breadth was designed by the British, who had planned a series of broad avenues radiating out from a central core — **Place de France,** where you will begin the Fourth Walk. Look to your left beyond Marcus Street: the hills in the distance always remain in view; one never forgets the mountains beyond, even in this urbane setting. Although the British Government was never able to carry the grand plan to completion, the streets that it built in Jerusalem are a unique contribution and stand in marked contrast to the narrow lanes of earlier — and even later — development.

Continue uphill on **Jabotinsky Street.** On your left is an imposing white-stone building rising above a double row of walls: **The Van Leer Foundation** and **Israel Academy of Arts and Science.** It is the work and meeting place for Israel's "brain trust."

Climb the driveway and enter the main building. Walk up the ramp on your right that leads to the back of the sitting area. Beyond it there is a long porch and from its far right end you can peek into the backyard of the **President's Residence.** This might be the moment to catch the President's children frolicking on the presidential lawn. The stained glass windows of the manor house reception hall are in clear view.

From this porch you can see the area that you will be visiting on this walk. Just ahead is the wildly convoluted roof of the **Jerusalem Theater.** The heavily wooded hill on the horizon at your left marks the location of the United Nations Command Headquarters on the **Hill of Evil Counsel.**

The wide-angled view recalls the Biblical description of Jerusalem as a city built on and surrounded by mountains. From every high place in the City you can see into a valley and beyond to other high places set off by other valleys. Residential neighborhoods are constructed on the tops of the hills; valleys are reserved for open space and circulation and are the blood stream of the city.

Those red roofs to your left top the houses of the German Colony and you will be heading toward them as you continue this walk, albeit on a rather circuitous route.

Return to Jabotinsky Street, turn left and walk over to the front gate of the President's residence, designed by Bezalel Schatz. You are now on **Ha-nassi Street.** If you have arrived at an auspicious moment you may see a military guard of honor standing at attention as a newly arrived diplomat comes to present his credentials.

The summit of the Hill of Evil Counsel.
The lonely tree now has many leafy companions.

The elderly President Shazar was in office when the building plans for the President's residence were presented for approval to the government. Navon, then Knesset Member, argued against approval of the building on the grounds that it would be expensive and impractical. During the floor debate he stated that one day a president with children might occupy the building and no provision had been made in the plans for such an eventuality. And indeed, in 1978 the interior spaces of the residence had to be redesigned to accommodate President Navon's own children.

If you are from America and think that all president's homes should resemble the White House, you will be surprised to find, as you continue to walk past this one, that a number of ordinary families live just five yards away and can look into the President's windows from theirs.

You are sauntering for just a moment on the outskirts of a neighborhood known as **Kiryat Shmuel** which was, at the time of the 1948 War of Independence, the western edge of the city. Just ahead, at

Shneurson Square, you are standing about 50 yards from the spot where the United Nation's Count Folke Bernadotte was assassinated by a terrorist band in 1948.

Follow the road as it turns left and cross over to the large, irregularly shaped rose-stone building on the other side of the street. This is the **Museum of Islamic Art,** open Monday, Tuesday and Thursday from 10 to 12:30 and from 3:30 to 6; Wednesday from 3:30 to 9 and Saturday from 10:30 to 1; closed on Fridays and holidays. This is a "must" museum, easy on the feet and a feast for the eyes. Don't miss the exquisite clock museum on the lower floor, or the Persian rugs on the upper floors.

When you are finished touring the museum cross the road at the zebra stripes. You are now on **Chopin Street,** walking behind the presidential residence and the Van Leer Foundation. Look up at the dove sitting on top of the obelisk just ahead and twirling around with an olive branch in his mouth. He, too, is looking into the President's windows.

The huge structure on your left is the **Jerusalem Theater,** which you are approaching from the back. To be properly impressed, go around to the front entrance plaza where you can see the outdoor sculpture by Yechiel Shemi and have a cup of coffee under a shade umbrella, something which, by now, you richly deserve. The sculpture is one of many that have been acquired by the Municipality for placement outdoors among the neighborhoods of the city so that even non-museum goers can have the pleasures of art-viewing with none of the strains.

If you have not made plans to attend an evening concert, ballet or play or a Friday afternoon movie, walk over to the box office on the right side of the plaza and immediately choose something you would like to see. If tickets are not available for the right performance at the right time, wander through the lobby and visit the art gallery to see the works of new-immigrant Israeli artists. (By the way, the bathrooms here are clean and well-appointed; you might not find any others till the end of your walk.)

The famous Begin-Sadat press conference took place here in November 1977. Israelis cannot forget that their Ministry of Communications was then able to set up a vast telephone system in this building, in less than 48 hours, which linked Israel to almost all of the countries in the world -- while some have been waiting for a home telephone for many years.

A flashback from the Jerusalem Theater outdoor cafe
to an anonymous Jerusalem street cafe in the 1800's

When you leave the theater turn left and start your stroll through the neighborhood called **Talbieh.** You need only look at the first building on your left, with blue-tile facade and burst of bougainvillea 14 yards high, to know that this neighborhood was originally built and populated by the wealthiest of Arab Jerusalemites.

You are walking on **Marcus Street**; at the second intersecting street on your right, cross it and enter **Hovevei Zion Street**, "the lovers of

Zion." Martin Buber used to live at No. 3. The Jerusalem Historical Society meets at No. 4.

The entire length of this quiet, residential street is lined with homes built in the style associated with gracious middle-eastern living: intricate stonework, enamel tiles, building blocks of rose-gold hue, and gardens so lavishly planted that one can barely distinguish the boundaries between them.

Notice the classic designs of the iron grillework on fences, balconies and gates, for which Arab craftsmen were justifiedly famous, and contrast them with the grillework used on the three or four modern buildings on the street. The contrast between old forms and new is particularly apparent at No. 12, where two modern floors were added onto the original one-story building.

The stone walls of all of the older buildings are extremely thick. Such walls provide superb insulation against the feared heat but are worse than useless against the damp and cold of a Jerusalem winter.

When you reach the foot of Hovevei Zion, which runs only three short blocks, you are suddenly in another world of open spaces, imposing landmarks spread out upon the rolling hills and a jumble of modern, tall (more than three stories, that is) apartment buildings clambering amongst themselves for a share of the view.

Turn right into **Yitzhaq Elhanan Street.** In two short blocks the road will curve to the right and pass the **Omariya Tower** and continue to the **Rose Garden** which can be entered from **Pinsker Street.** If this is springtime many varieties of magnificent roses will be on display; during other seasons there will be a fair sampling of indigenous flowering plants. Rest, then leave the garden through the Pinsker entrance, turn right and follow the road as it curves to the right and then to the left into a street called **Eli Graetz.** Look to the left for occasional but tantalizing views of the walls of the Old City and the Church of the Dormition on Mount Zion.

Turn right at the first intersection. You are now walking through the **German Colony,** a neighborhood founded by German settlers in 1874. They called themselves the Templars, for the Temple was the symbol of their attachment to Jerusalem. During the Second World War the British removed the entire German population of this colony to another Germany colony and kept them confined until the end of the war when many of them migrated to Australia. The British took over their homes and declared the entire area "off-limits." When the neighborhood was conquered by Israeli soldiers during the War of Independence, it became Jewish and the German church was handed over to the Armenians who had been cut off from their own church in the Old City when the City was divided into two separate parts.

Most of the buildings on this part of the walk have been designated as landmarks for preservation. Be sure to peek into the private gardens along the way; they are typical Jerusalem gardens -- no well-defined beds of flowers, no manicured lawns, only luxuriant growth wherever a bit of earth can be stocked with seed.

You are now walking along **Dor Dor Vedorshav Street.** At the corner is **Mohliver Street.** On your left is the **Museum of Natural History,** which is open Sunday through Thursday from 10 to 1, on Monday and Wednesday from 4 to 6 also, and on the Sabbath from 10:30 to 1.

After your visit to the museum continue walking along Mohliver Street. Notice that the shapes of the houses are extremely simple --- a stone box with a tile roof and heavy wrought iron gates and window bars. Here you will find little of your Jerusalem frippery -- arched windows, carved columns or filigree in stone. The windows are square and solid, burgher-like, if you will. But there is the softening effect of bougainvillea everywhere.

Turn left at the bottom of Mohliver Street. At this point one can note that not all of the neighborhood is quaint and solid. There is ample evidence that several immigrant families have been housed in buildings originally meant for single-family dwellings. Contrast the buildings around the courtyard at No. 15 with the buildings you saw earlier on this walk to gain an understanding of the deterioration that results from over-crowding. This is a common phenomenon in the older neighborhoods of Jerusalem — the wealthy and the poor living side by side in old buildings, the former because they are beautiful and spacious, the latter because they have no choice.

This street, **Hamagid,** turns to the right and enters a major thoroughfare, **Emek Refaim.** This is the "main drag" of the German Colony; in the days of the Bible the area was noted as the principal agricultural district outside the city of Jerusalem. It is particularly famous as the battlefield where David fought the Philistines.

Cross Emek Refaim Street — carefully! — turn left and enter **Lloyd George Street,** which is typical of the Germany Colony. Notice how some of the new buildings jar their older neighbors.

At the first intersection turn left again, into **Jan Smuts Street** (the British were very careful to cover up any traces of the German origins of this community) and then left again into **Cremieux Street.** At No. 8 there is another staircase leading up to someone's unrealized plan to add a second floor to his home. The courtyard at No. 4 is particularly charming.

You are now back on **Emek Refaim Street.** At No. 6 you will see the first house built in the German Colony. Next to it is the second oldest house in the neighborhood and on its threshold is a quote in German from the *Book of Isaiah*: "Arise, shine: for thy light is come and the glory of the Lord is risen upon thee."

Continue on Emek Refaim. Across the street there is an unusual example of a German church. You will soon pass a large gas station. Right next to it is the **Liberty Bell Park**, Jerusalem's newest and boldest public playground. As of this writing the entrance path from the main road has not as yet been completed, so you will have to walk into the park without specific directions. All paths will lead you to the main arbor, a green and growing arcade lighting the way to a replica of the Liberty Bell. Branching out from the arcade are small activity areas where you may challenge an old-timer to a chess game on a stone table, watch a high school drama group rehearsing its current offering, see a father and son flying kites, or listen to the chamber group playing in the amphitheater. There is also a place for a light snack before you leave the park at its exit on **Jabotinsky Street** where another No. 15 bus will take you back to the center of town.

*The houses in the German Colony in Haifa 100 years ago:
as neat and solid as the stone boxes in Jerusalem's Colony*

THE FOURTH WALK

FROM PLACE DE FRANCE TO THE
CRAFTSMAN'S COURTYARD

This walk follows a winding route through another of Jeru-
salem's elegant neighborhoods and finally reaches a section of
the Old City Walls which you have not yet visited. Along the
way you will find painters, sculptors, weavers, and enough
modern jewelry stores and antique shops to satisfy the appe-
tites of the most ardent window-shoppers. Lest the things of
this world be too much for you, there are also visits to
off-the-beaten-track religious institutions where attempts are
made to promote an ongoing dialogue between Moslem, Jew
and Christian. For added variety you will be passing through
a Moslem cemetery, Jerusalem's first attempt at "urban
renewal" and a museum devoted to the subject of taxes. It
opens at 1 in the afternoon, so if you set out at about 12
noon you can manage a visit there and still get to the Crafts-
man's Courtyard before it closes at 4 in the afternoon, but
don't forget your hat.

Five roads lead into the **Place de France: Keren Hayesod** from the
western side of the Old City: **Agron** from its northwest corner, **King
George** from the Central Business District; **Gaza Road** and **Ramban
Street** leading from the Hebrew University that lies in the exact center of the New City. Start this walk in front of **Terra Sancta**, the only
building on the square which is entirely surrounded by a wrought-iron

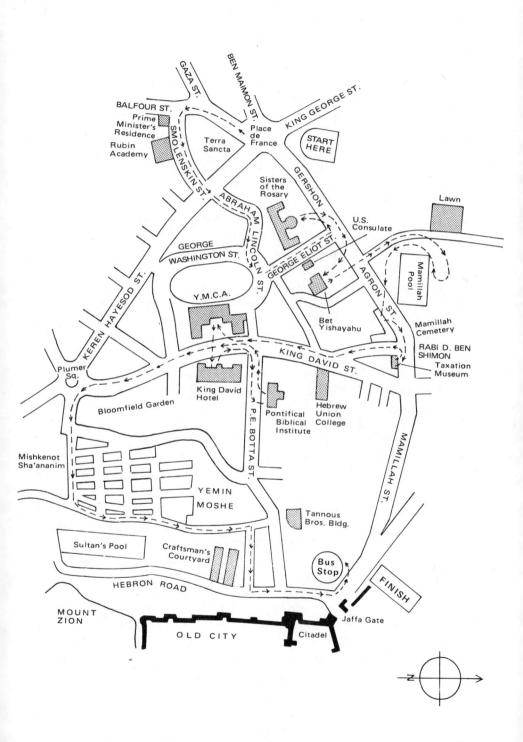

GAZA ST.

BEN MAIMON ST.

KING GEORGE ST.

BALFOUR ST.

Prime
Minister's
Residence

Rubin
Academy

Terra
Sancta

SMOLENSKIN ST.

Place
de
France

START
HERE

GERSHON

Sisters
of the
Rosary

Lawn

ABRAHAM LINCOLN ST.

U.S.
Consulate

GEORGE ELIOT ST.

GEORGE
WASHINGTON ST.

KEREN HAYESOD ST.

Y.M.C.A.

Bet
Yishayahu

Mamillah
Pool

AGRON ST.

Mamillah
Cemetery

RABI D. BEN
SHIMON

Taxation
Museum

Plumer
Sq.

King David
Hotel

KING DAVID ST.

Bloomfield Garden

P.E. BOTTA ST.

Pontifical
Biblical
Institute

Hebrew
Union
College

MAMILLAH ST.

Mishkenot
Sha'ananim

YEMIN

MOSHE

Tannous
Bros. Bldg.

Sultan's Pool

Craftsman's
Courtyard

Bus
Stop

FINISH

HEBRON ROAD

MOUNT
ZION

OLD CITY

Citadel

Jaffa Gate

N

fence. It was originally a college operated by the Franciscan Fathers and in 1948 it became the temporary home of the Hebrew University, when the Mount Scopus campus could no longer be used and the Givat Ram campus had not yet been divided up among prospective donors. Walk along the side of the building opposite the **Discount Bank**. You are now entering **Talbieh**, formerly a wealthy Arab-Jewish neighborhood, now a well-to-do Jewish one. Soon you will pass a large billboard pasted full of notices of the coming attractions in Jerusalem. Read them carefully, or, rather, hunt for clues among the scattered English words; some of the events advertised here never get into the newspapers or tourist pamphlets.

Keep the Terra Sancta fence firmly on your left as you follow the bends of this road to the intersection with **Smolenskin Street**, where there is a residential building surrounded by a stone wall. This is the official **Residence of the Prime Minister**. A guard is stationed here twenty-four hours per day. Turn left into Smolenskin Street. Next to the Prime Minister's home is the **Rubin Academy of Music**, which houses a museum of musical instruments. Open daily from 10 to 1.

Continue down Smolenskin to **Keren Hayesod Street**. The building on the near, right-hand corner is an example of typical building development in this neighborhood. The first floors of the building were constructed by a wealthy Arab family for private use. But because land is terribly expensive in this desirable location, it became necessary to use almost every available rooftop for further construction. The original structure — the lower level — can be distinguished from the additions above by the different stonework.

Cross Keren Hayesod and enter **Abraham Lincoln Street** (pronounced with the second "l" intact). You are now passing through a typical middle-class neighborhood of Jerusalem. As required by law, all buildings in Jerusalem must be made of stone. Keep your eye on the overhanging porches. Families in Jerusalem like to invest in old Turkish and Persian rugs. Some of them are treasures, and all of them are taken out daily for a solid thumping, a holdover from the days when there were no vacuum cleaners. You will notice that often these porches are bulging with bedding. Jerusalem housewives air their bedding daily, in the belief that there is no cleansing and sterilizing agent as effective as the Jerusalem sun. At No. 9 Lincoln there is a small grocery store (*makolet*) tucked under the stairwell. Go in and browse around to see what products are available to the local housekeeper.

Soon Lincoln Street will twist off to your right. Keep following it. The wall you see before you is the property boundary of the **Y.M.C.A.** and the place where Abe Lincoln and George Washington meet and then separate, as history demands, one going left, the other right. The barbed wire has no dramatic military significance — it merely prevents gate-crashers from climbing over the wall to see the weekly soccer games at the "Y" free of charge.

Soon Lincoln will meet **George Eliot Street.** Walk its length to **Gershon Agron Street.** Turn to your left for about a hundred yards to see one of the most beautiful buildings in Jerusalem — the home of the **Sisters of the Rosary.** A low, round white building, it has a number of small circular wings, and getting into it will require a determined effort on your part. You may not succeed, but it is worth a try. The Sisters are a teaching and missionary order. Their school is the large, rectangular wing to the right of the round building; here children from East Jerusalem learn their lessons.

Turn right outside the Mission yard. Just past Eliot Street you will see another tall stone wall with a heavy, black iron gate. This is the official **residence of the American Consul-General.** Press your nose against the gate to get a slimpse of the Arabian night-like building and gardens.

Continue down Agron until you come to another large garden with a small building tucked inside. This is **Bet Yeshayahu** (the House of Isaiah). The garden is a bit jumbled, but it contains five of the seven types of produce described in the Bible as typical of the Land of Israel — as much as is milk and honey. There are one fig, one pomegranate and several olive trees, a patch of wheat, and a grape arbor — with nontraditional artichoke plants for a fillip. Walk into the secretariat and tell them you would like to find out about their work. Bet Yeshayahu is the headquarters of a Dominican Order whose purpose is to explore the Judaic roots of Christianity. One of the fathers is a teacher at the Hebrew University, another, an authorized guide to Jerusalem. All of them are very much involved in establishing a continuing dialogue between Jews and Christians and ultimately with Moslems as well. Ask to see their simple and lovely place of worship. All of their services are conducted in Hebrew. The church fittings have all been designed or executed by the sculptor Palombo who designed the iron Knesset gates and whose museum you visited on Mount Zion. One of the truly great treasures to be seen in the church is a set of the Bible published in the 1600's, each page printed in seven different languages.

In this short stretch of **Agron Street** you have seen three foreign institutions, each attracted to Jerusalem for quite different purposes.

Now, cross Agron to **Gan Ha'atzma'ut** (Independence Park). You will find a path leading into the interior of the park, where there is a large lawn, the favorite sporting grounds of the "drop-out" segment of Jerusalem's youthful population. Rest here. It's a good place for striking up conversations. Then retrace your steps on the main pathway and take the second left turn off the path to the barbed wire enclosure of **Mamillah Pool.** Its origins are in the very distant past, but in its present form the pool was built by Sultan Suleiman, the master builder of Jerusalem in the middle 1500's, as a catchment basin for rain-water. Since the pool is on a higher level than the Old City, in the Middle Ages water flowed by gravitation from the reservoir to the consumer. There is a nineteenth-century picture of the pool showing people swimming about, indicating that even then they knew all about multiple-use reservoirs. Walk the full length of the pool (keep it on your left) and you will find yourself in the middle of an old Moslem cemetery. Walk down the narrow path between the graves. You will see examples of traditional Moslem tombstones, with double headstones and graceful inscriptions. It is difficult to determine the meaning of the double head-stone: could it represent a "husband and wife facing each other across the breakfast table," as suggested by Dennis Silk?

When you reach an exceptionally wide, tall eucalyptus tree, turn right and walk down the short flight of stone steps to Agron Street. Cross the street and look at the building of fine Arab design which is now the home of the **Ministry of Commerce and Industry.** In its prime it was an elegant Arab hotel — the Palace. Then the first floor was an arcade, its open spaces defined by the graceful pointed arches of the main floor; now it has been closed up to make more office space. (Then the arcade held a fine coffeehouse — now, coffee is made only at the ten o'clock break.) The pointed, arched windows and the heavy orna-mentation are typical of turn-of-the-century public buildings in this part of the world. The designs that jut out of the building face are based on motifs characteristic of a much earlier period of Saracen archi-tecture. You may want to have a look at the extravagant staircase inside.

Walk to the building at the corner of **Rabi David Ben Shimon Street.** The display cases on the outside of the building house some of the exhibits of the **Taxation Museum.** By all means, look around the

*The Mamillah Pool and the Moslem Cemetery when Jerusalemites had
more leisure time than they have today*

museum itself; there are only two other taxation museums in the world.
Like nothing else of its kind in Israel, it is open during the siesta
hours — 1 to 4 in the afternoon.

Take Rabi David Ben Shimon Street directly into **King David
Street.** The handsome white building on the opposite side of the street
is the **Hebrew Union College,** founded by the Reform Movement in
Judaism, based in Cincinnati. If you feel the need for a breather at this
point, wander through its gardens and rest on one of the stone stools.
(Come back during Saturday morning services at 10 for a more extensive visit.)

You will pass some lovely and some less lovely shops on King
David as you walk to the **Y.M.C.A.** This building is a superb example of a modern adaptation of older architectural forms. Walk through
its arcaded galleries and you will be carried back to Scheherezade. On
the floor of the entranceway there is a reproduction of the famous
Madeba Map, found in a mosaic floor of the fourth century. From it,
scholars have learned a great deal about Roman and Byzantine Jerusalem. The Y.M.C.A. Tower contains the highest observation point in
the area, and from it there are unparalleled views of Jerusalem to the
north, south, east and west. You can ride in an elevator to the tower
in two minutes at a small fee but climbing is even cheaper. (The Tower

is open daily from 9 to 6; closed on Sunday.) Be sure to look at the huge carillon that can be heard throughout Jerusalem before each Christian holiday. (Another Saturday morning treat in Jerusalem is the Y.M.C.A. organ concert at 11:30.)

Cross the street to the **King David Hotel**, where you can stop for a snack at the coffee shop. Outside the hotel, turn right and walk a half-block to **Paul Emile Botta Street**. Enter this street and walk about two hundred yards until you come to a building on your left which is set in a fine landscaped garden. The **Pontifical Biblical Institute** is another excellent example of the gracious architecture of former times, when the labor of experienced stonemasons was inexpensive and easily obtained. Note the upper story of this building. Its open arcade, typical of the Middle East, is designed to keep the sun out and bring in any passing breeze. Enter the building and ask to be shown their museum. Although the pieces are ancient — there is even a mummy — the exhibit itself is not as interesting as is the manner in which the caretaker shows off its treasures. The caretaker will also take you into the library, sponsored by the Vatican, where you can browse undisturbed in air-conditioned bliss through some fine books about Jerusalem, or anything else that catches your fancy.

Leave the Institute and walk past the King David Hotel. That is **Bloomfield Garden** on your left and its major attraction, a circle of stone pillars with no apparent function, is known locally and fondly as Stonehenge. Turn left into the tree-lined road at the traffic light. At the end of the road a short flight of stone steps will lead you down to the **Windmill**. It was constructed in 1857 by Sir Moses Montefiore as part of his effort to encourage Jews to leave the confines of the Old City and create a new life outside its walls. Contrary to Sir Moses' hopes, the Windmill never did become the industrial foundation of a new life for those Jews who came to settle outside the Old City. Some say that the winds here were never strong enough to turn the vanes. But its usefulness in helping newcomers figure out where they are cannot be questionned. Stop for a moment to see the carriage on the right of the stairs which bears the Montefiore coat of arms. It was designed to include the word Jerusalem in Hebrew letters, and such letters were not a common sight in the England of the 1800's.

On the wall outside the carriage house you will find a ceramic mural dedicated to Sir Montefiore who "strived and worked for the Land of Israel, the father of the neighborhoods outside the walls of Jerusalem, encouraged agriculture and industry, fought for the rights of the Jews in Exile." The mural was created by Leah Majora Mintz, whose clay sculptures of naked ladies are included as one of the attractions of the Eighth Walk.

Walk to the southeastern edge of the platform on which you are standing. Ahead of you is Mount Zion with the black-coned roof and the belfry of the Church of the Dormition dominating the skyline. The Valley of Hinnom lies at the bottom of the Mount Zion slope, below the road.

The village rising on the other side of the valley opposite Mount Zion is **Abu-Tor**, which was divided into a Jewish and Arab section by a concrete wall representing the Armistice Line established after the 1948 War of Independence. **St. Andrew's Church** is the white-domed massive structure off to your right, and the hills of Judea in Jordan line the horizon.

Turn left and walk to the staircase adjoining this platform, **Yemin Moshe Street.** It divides the area into the residential neighborhood of **Yemin Moshe** on the left and the public buildings of **Mishkenot Sha'ananim** (Dwellings of Serenity) on the right.

Mishkenot consists of two narrow one-story buildings, the lower of the two being very long indeed. The shorter, higher one is the **Jerusalem Music Center;** the lower one, a hotel reserved exclusively for artists from all over the world who are invited here by the Municipality to work and vacation. The Jerusalem Music Center was founded by the Mayor of Jerusalem and the violinist Isaac Stern. Well-known musicians come here, whenever their concert schedules permit it, to work with young students of music. Their teaching sessions are taped and played back to other students. Sometimes these audio-visual tapes find their way to the television stations and provide an incredible treat for the rest of the country.

Follow the sign that says Mishkenot Sha'ananim to the lower building and enter the lobby of the hotel. Notice how carefully the building has been restored to protect and isolate the working artists. Perhaps you will be allowed to go down the stairs to investigate the entrance corridor leading to each of the private apartments. And maybe you will see Saul Bellow or someone else of his like in the lobby scribbling notes for another book on Jerusalem.

Return to Yemin Moshe Street, walk down the staircase and turn **right** just before the sign reading "Mishkenot Sha'ananim Restaurant,"

*Mishkenot Sha'ananim with the protective enclosure
that no longer exists*

to take a better look at Mishkenot, which was the very first Jewish
settlement built outside the Wall. Sir Moses, appalled by the overcrowded conditions in the Jewish Quarter, tried to persuade the residents to settle outside the Old City. He was aided by a bequest of
funds from Judah Touro, a New Orleans businessman. Knowing the
dangers of leaving a protected environment, Sir Moses built Mishkenot
as a fortress — it was once entirely surrounded by a wall — its roof
made in the form of the ramparts of the Old City Wall. He envisioned
this as an integrated community and so provided sixteen apartments,
eight for *Sephardim* and eight for *Ashkenazim*. (Ashkenazim are Jews
from Western countries; Sephardim originally came from Spain and
migrated to other lands after their expulsion in 1492. The two groups
have not always lived together amicably.) As a special inducement, he
offered sums of money to anyone willing to live in this new community. There were takers, but — unknown to him — the first residents
lived here only during the day, and at the first signs of the setting of the
sun, they rushed quickly back to their old homes within the Walls
before the Zion Gate was locked for the night. This was all back in the
1860's.

As you walk down Mishkenot, notice the pipes holding up the overhanging roof. They were provided by Sir Montefiore, who, it appears

did not trust Palestinian industry, for the name of the English factory that manufactured them is still there. Legitimate lack of trust also motivated the restorers of this old building when, in the early 1970's, they sealed the original entrances to the apartments to protect the artists at work from prying eyes, such as yours and mine, and from unwanted entries.

Walk back to the main staircase. It forms the southern boundary of **Yemin Moshe,** which you are about to enter.

Constructed some 30 years after Mishkenot, when the idea of leaving the Old City was not quite as unacceptable as it had been a generation or so before, Yemin Moshe was nonetheless among the earliest settlements to be built outside the walls. Jews left the Old City to settle in Yemin Moshe and Mishkenot, and because history is known to play tricks on man, it was from these same settlements that they moved forward in an attempt to retake the Jewish Quarter of the Old City during the War of Independence. The settlement rises on a mountain slope, with four rows of housing, each on separate ascending levels. Each row is bisected four times by stone staircases rising from the lowest level to the highest. At the foot of each staircase there is an iron gate, which was formerly locked each night. For maximum protection, none of the doors of the individual houses open to the outside, but rather onto the narrow interior lanes.

Walk into the typical Yemin Moshe lane that begins opposite the Mishkenot Sha'ananim Restaurant. (An excellent place for lunch and dinner, provided you are very solvent.) This is **Ha-mevasser Street,** which runs north and south and separates two rows of housing. At the first opening on your left is a staircase partially covered by an irregularly shaped arch supporting an overhanging connection between two buildings. Watch your step as you walk up the narrow and steep staircase.

You are in the heart of Yemin Moshe, and since you now know that no matter in what direction you walk — north or south, up or down — you will come to the outer edge of the settlement, feel free to roam around. Notice how many of the buildings have been, or are in the process of being, extensively rehabilitated. Many of the old houses have been bought by artists who have converted them into studios, salesrooms, and living quarters.

This is Jerusalem's first experiment with urban renewal. As in all urban renewal areas, the human problems have been perhaps more difficult to solve than the physical ones. Yemin Moshe had been a community of immigrant Jews from Persia and Turkey who settled here in the 1950's on the edge of "no man's land," because they had no choice. For twenty years they were fair game for the Arab Legionnaires who manned the ramparts of the Old City Wall opposite. These people could not afford to undertake the extensive renovation work required by the Municipality when the no-man's land became a garden. Their homes were sold by lottery to people who could afford "beautification" and they themselves were provided with new apartments in different neighborhoods of the City.

In order to restore the community to its original state, building codes were enacted which stipulated that all modern appurtenances, such as water pipes and electric lines which did not exist in 1893, must be removed from sight; water gutters on the roofs must be newly enclosed with wood; all asbestos lean-tos must be torn down and plumbing and gaslines must be placed within the buildings or underground; the old stones must be cleaned and new filler added. Some handsome solutions have been found to these restoration problems.

When you have finished your explorations, work your way down to the bottom of the nearest staircase. There you will find a narrow road bordering the eastern rim of this community and its main entrance, an iron gate with a Star of David carved into the stone. A stone tablet above the gate announces that this community was named for Sir Moses Montefiore (Moses is the English equivalent of the Hebrew name Moshe) and its main street after his wife Yehudit, both of whom contributed large amounts of money and time to develop Jewish settlement all over Palestine.

On the other side of the road there is a deep gorge in the earth which was once a water-filled pool. Although this pool was originally built in the days of the Second Temple, its name, the **Sultan's Pool**, derives from Suleiman the Magnificent. In the sixteenth century, this Ottoman-Turkish ruler (who, as you recall, also built the wall surrounding the Old City) rebuilt the pool on the remains of a previous construction by the Crusaders in the twelfth century, who had used it to water their horses. The Sultan, who was a most clever city-builder, knew that Jerusalem could never again be a great city, as it had formerly been, without an assured water supply. His architects knew that the Valley of Hinnom acts as a natural conduit for rainwater. The valley begins at the marketplace of Mahane Yehudah, runs down Jaffa

Road to Zion Square, where it turns right into Mamillah Pool, where you just were, curves around to the walls of the Old City, and follows them to the Valley of Kidron on the east side of the city. There the waters of both valleys meet and flow out to the Dead Sea. In order to prevent the loss of this water source, the Sultan built a dam, which is the stone wall you see at the far end of the gorge, and enlarged the pool. (You crossed the dam on your way to Mount Zion on the Second Walk in this book.)

Follow the road as it slopes downward toward two long low buildings with terraced roofs. These twin buildings are called **Khutsot Hayotzer**, "Craftsman's Courtyard," the arcaded marketplace of the artisan.

James Felt Lane lies between the two buildings — follow it for a visit to the studios and salesrooms of a number of Jerusalem craftsmen. You will see glassblowers, silversmiths, ceramicists and weavers at work. The studios are open from 10 to 4.

Then, have a cup of coffee on the rooftop terrace where you can enjoy a magnificent view into the Valley of Hinnom.

Turn left on the road outside Khutsot Hayotzer that parallels the Old City Wall. Just about at the point where this street meets another street coming in from the left, you will be standing opposite the **Citadel**, distinguished by its tall narrow tower, known locally — and incorrectly — as the **Tower of David**. Actually, the Citadel has five towers and is, in fact, an elegant defensive system that has been enlarged, restored and rebuilt over the ages by every conqueror of Jerusalem — except King David. Notice the steep slope — technically termed, "glacis" — leading up from the valley to the wall. Any enemy who wanted to scale the wall had first to reach the top of the rise. But, having achieved this difficult task, he would find no level place from which to begin an assault on the wall itself, and so the entire effort would fail. In fact, the way in which topography was used to build the Old City was so successful at this point that although Jerusalem was conquered again and again throughout its history, no invader ever succeeded in taking it from this western side.

Between the end of the wall of the Citadel and the beginning of the City Wall you will see a narrow cleft cutting into the "glacis." This was at one time part of a deep, dry moat that completely encircled the Citadel, both inside and outside the Old City. Eighty years ago the paved open entrance to the Old City that you see on your left was part of this deep chasm. At this point you can see that the Citadel Wall and the Old City Wall are not connected. Should an invader succeed in scaling the Wall of Jerusalem, he would have had to repeat the process in order to conquer the Citadel, which was planned as the City's "last stand."

This ancient moat was filled in and paved in 1892, when Kaiser Wilhelm II of Germany paid a state visit to Palestine and would not consider entering the City except on his white horse with full ceremonial retinue. Since Jaffa Gate itself was too narrow for such a procession the moat was filled in and paved.

Notice the square stone boxes that jut out of the Citadel Wall. They are machicouli, common features on all the gates and on various sections of the Wall as well. A defender could enter the box from the ramparts of the Wall to pour hot oil or any other weapon on the enemy below, while he himself remained entirely concealed and protected.

The Armistice Line that, until 1967, separated Jerusalem into "East" and "West" ran from the sharp corner of the Old City Wall on the far right, down the "glacis" in a line veering toward the left, through the middle of the two long, low buildings of the Craftsman's Courtyard, then far to the left and upward into the parking area for buses. Everything around your own position was formerly "no man's land." Follow the road leading away from the Old City Wall toward some very decrepit-looking stone buildings, with laundry hanging out in front. Only in your imagination can the former elegance of these turn-of-the-century buildings be recaptured. In the early 1900's Jaffa Gate was the commercial center of the city and the preferred location for every shopkeeper. The lower floors of these old buildings were fine shops, the upper floors, elegant dwellings. But no building on the edge of a "no man's land" can retain commercial value, and after the '48 Armistice, the old stores were converted into garages and workshops for light industry; some even became housing. Who was willing to live in such dangerous quarters for almost twenty years? The original Arab owners fled at the beginning of the War of Independence and no sooner had they fled than their houses were occupied by Jewish refugees pouring into Israel from Arab lands. Even a cursory glance at the dominant **Tannous Building** will reveal something of the difficult conditions under which these refugees lived. The marks of artillery shells are clearly visible. The windows on the lower floor were bricked in, except for the narrow apertures provided with iron shutters. For twenty years the upper story served as an Israeli Army military position. There was some concern that the occupants of these buildings would be unwilling to remain in their homes if the military situation became heated along the Armistice Line. However, not a single resident fled, even at the outbreak of the Six-Day War.

This entire area is included in a controversial development plan prepared for the City by the Architect Safdie. The Mamillah Plan provides for underground parking, a new road system, luxury apartment buildings and arcaded shopping streets; in fact, all the appurtenances of 20th century elegance.

In the meantime, and until this plan is executed, the large bus-parking area nearby will continue to be shoddy but that's where the No. 18 bus is parked that will take you back to the center of town.

THE FIFTH WALK

FROM ZION SQUARE TO ME'A SHE'ARIM

This walk starts at Zion Square in the heart of town. It will take you through one of the first neighborhoods developed outside the walled Old City; into the Israeli law courts; past some interesting churches established by priests in very foreign garb; into two museums, one representing the "ploughshare," the other, the "sword"; down one of the City's most beautiful streets, its entire length just one block; and finally into the City's "second walled city." You will not be allowed to enter if you are dressed immodestly: knee-length dresses with covering on the upper arms for females, long pants for the gents. This walk should be taken only during the morning or early afternoon hours since the two museums included in it close at approximately 4 in the afternoon. If you start out at about 10:45 you will be able to hear part of the mass at the Russian Orthodox Church as well as the two o'clock Ethiopian services, with time out for lunch in between.

Most bus routes go into the center of town and have stops close to **Zion Square**. Start your walk on the southeast corner of the square where there is a large semicircular sidewalk. On your right, as you face the square, there is a narrow street named **Yoel Moshe Salmon** with sidewalks surely no wider than 3 feet. You are entering one of those semi-

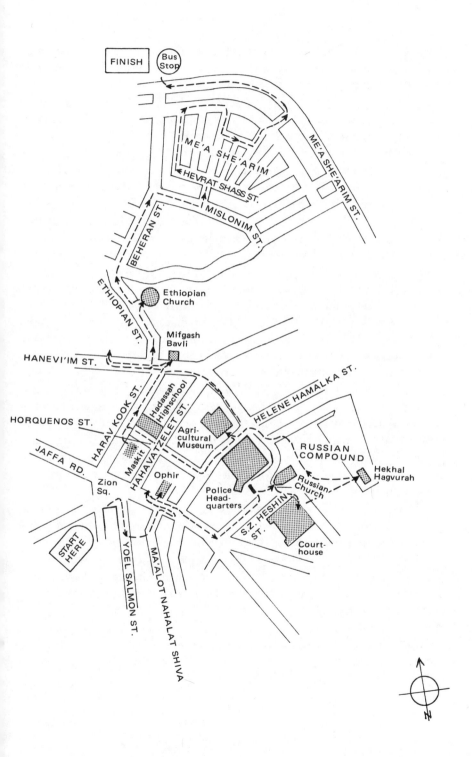

dilapidated old neighborhoods commonly found in the centers of large cities all over the world. Its name: **Nahalat Shiva**. But before you enter this street look toward the opposite side of Jaffa Road and at the second intersecting side street (**Hahavatzelet Street**); you will see a number of elderly men either sitting or reclining on the pavement. They are from Kurdistan, Iraq, and their trade is handed down from father to son. They are porters, waiting for someone to tap them on the shoulder and offer them a day's work. It is a highly informal labor exchange.

Nahalat Shiva (The Estate of the Seven) was built more than 100 years ago, and was the second settlement founded outside the walls of the Old City. (You saw the first — Mishkenot Sha'ananim — on your fourth walk in Jerusalem.) When Nahalat Shiva was built in the 1860's, there were few buildings on either side of Jaffa Road, even though then, as today, it served as the main road between Jerusalem and the major coastal cities (Jaffa in those days, Tel Aviv today). In contrast to Mishkenot Sha'ananim, which was founded by foreign philanthropists, Nahalat Shiva built by the settlers themselves, all former residents of the Old City. The seven pioneering families, all of them Orthodox Jews, met with opposition from the Old City's leaders, who argued that the true and holy Jerusalem lay within the ancient walls only and that, therefore, there could never be a "new" Jerusalem. They were wrong, of course, but then they were not aware of the fact that the contours of the walls of Jerusalem were different in each period of history, which means that the real Jerusalem cannot be confined to one specific place. Precise information on the various locations of the walls of Jerusalem have become known only within the past 100 years through intensive archaeological explorations.

After Nahalat Shiva became a going concern, the original settlers left it and pioneered other new communities, Me'a She'arim and Petah Tikva. Now, the neighborhood is awaiting the arrival of its own urban restorer, who is, at present writing, nameless. That person will have to strip off the blight to reveal the basic charm of this area. Perhaps you will be able to uncover it even without professional help. Others have -- enterprising young people who have opened coffee shops, boutiques and galleries along its narrow lanes. And some major city services are provided on Salmon Street by a polisher who keeps every Jerusalem family's copper collection glowing brightly, or a highly unique store selling goods made from rubber.

At No. 11 Salmon Street you will see an arched opening. Follow this lane to that dreadful white stone building whose corner juts out over an intersecting lane, **Ma'alot Nahalat Shiva**. Walk into the first courtyard on your left. Remember that courtyards in Mediterranean countries are a community's service and meeting place. Some of the houses are painted blue, a shade used widely in this part of the world to ward off the evil eye. A jerry-can is poised above an ivy-covered arbor — a makeshift shower contrived by people with no indoor plumbing.

Now, walk over to the adjoining courtyard which can be entered from No. 4 Ma'alot Nahalat Shiva. Look up at the overhanging terrace and you will see a long pipe running along its base till it reaches the ground. This pipe was used to catch rainwater and lead it underground to the cistern you see in the far left-hand corner of the paved yard. This was the community's sole source of water and when it failed, as in a year of light rainfall, water had to be imported by train from Jaffa. Notice the many wooden and metal lean-to's built onto the original structures. While these additions contribute their share to the general air of dilapidation, they in fact modernize the buildings, since they are the kitchens and bathrooms which were originally lacking. Notice the small unpaved plot with its large eucalyptus tree. A mean little space now, it was then of revolutionary importance for the early settlers of Nahalat Shiva who were eager to return to nature after their treeless existence in the Old City's Jewish Quarter.

Walk up the stone staircase at the end of Ma'alot Nahalat Shiva and look at the side of the modern building on your right, which contains three types of stone commonly found in Jerusalem. The flat white stone of the facade, although machine-finished, is the most expensive; the yellowish-pink, rough-edge stone that gives Jerusalem its golden tones is hand-carved but less expensive; and the cheapest of all is the gray, concrete imitation. This building is called **Bet Yoel** after one of the founders of Nahalat Shiva, for it stands on the site of the old settlement's first building.

You are now standing on **Jaffa Road**. Walk over the far corner of Bet Yoel and glance over at the opposite side of Jaffa Road. The buildings facing you are particularly fine examples of Arab architecture — of course, for the wealthy only. From this vantage point you can see one building on a side street off Jaffa Road that is heavily ornamented with fine blue and white enamel tiles, a favorite form of Islamic decoration.

The bottom of Jaffa Road as it was then

Retrace your steps on Jaffa Road to the nearest crossing equipped with a stoplight. On the opposite side of the street, at No. 38, you will find **Ophir**, an interesting jeweler in a tiny shop on the first landing. Antique jewelry, tiny treasures from the Roman period, some rings from Austro-Hungary, Persian miniatures, a piece of jade or two from Hong Kong, lie about in casual heaps. Avram, the master craftsman himself, knows where every piece is and will design and execute a fine new setting for any piece that catches your eye.

To your right on Jaffa Road is **Cafe Alaska**, selling the best sherbet Jerusalem has to offer. To your left, at No. 34, is the Municipal Tourist Information Office, equipped with smiling English-speaking women, who will answer your questions, give you maps and send you on your

way. They are open on Sundy through Thursday from 8 to 6, on
Friday only till 2.

Just ahead, Jaffa Road is divided in two by a large island of flowers.
In the days of the British this square was the hub of commercial life in
Jerusalem. When, in 1947, the conflict between the Jewish populace
and the ruling British Mandatory Government reached its peak, the area
was barricaded and only those with special permits could enter. Jewish
shopowners were forced to rebuild elsewhere, and the commercial center spread to the west and north.

Make a sharp left into **S.Z. Heshin Street.** You are about to enter
the **Russian Compound.** But before you do, stop at No. 1 Heshin to
buy a really splendid map of Jerusalem at the offices of the Department
of Surveys. (They are available in Hebrew and in English.)

The square before you including all of its buildings was constructed
by the Russian Orthodox Church to serve the needs of their pilgrims to
the Holy Land. After the Russian Revolution of 1917, when the Orthodox Church lost its official status, the property and buildings, except
for the Church itself and some housing for the few remaining clergymen, were sold to the British, who conquered Jerusalem during World
War I. The compound is built on an ancient rock quarry which supplied
the building stone for much of Second Temple Jerusalem. In the center of the square there is an ancient pillar abandoned in its bed of rock
by the stonemason who so carelessly caused the center crack. The
dimensions of the pillar have been found to coincide exactly with con-
temporaneous descriptions of the Basilica of the Second Temple.

On your left is the **Police Headquarters** and the remand jail; on your
right, the courthouse. Directly in front is the **Russian Church.** At its
entrance families can often be seen waiting for their imprisoned
relatives to be brought from the courts to the prison. Walk into the
church. Perhaps you will have come at the time of services. If not, and
the building is closed, ask a church official in the courthouse to let you
in. This building is the finest example of traditional Russian church
architecture to be seen in Israel.

As you leave the church, take the path on your left to reach the
entrance to the **Courts.** There is a Cyrillic engraving above the entrance
to the courthouse at No. 6. If your Hebrew is fairly good — it need not
be superb — listen to the sessions in any of the courtrooms on the main
floor. Hearing even the most minor case will give you some insight into
the workings of Israeli society. You will be amazed to see the judge

writing the testimony by hand. Court stenographers have not yet been
introduced into Israel. The Supreme Court also sits in this building, and
at times its hearings are disrupted by the roosters crowing in the farm-
yards of the Russians who continue to live on the lower floors of the
building.

As you leave the courthouse, walk straight ahead to the barbed wire
fence enclosing the compound of the **Palestine Central Prison,** used by
the British to hold captured members of "Lehi" and "Etzel," two of
the Jewish resistance groups during the time of the British Mandatory
rule in Palestine. Menahem Begin was formerly the leader of this
latter group. The Central Prison is now a museum called **Hekhal
Hagvurah** (Hall of Heroism). It is open daily from 9 to 3 and on Friday till 1; closed on Saturday. The long, low building on your right was
originally an inn for Russian pilgrims. Under British rule, its rooms were
converted into prison cells. Behind the entrance hall is the execution
chamber, with the gallows still in place. No Jew was ever executed in
Jerusalem for fear of the reaction among the Jewish population. All
Jews condemned to death were kept here until the day of their
appointed execution, which always took place in the Arab city of Acre.
On the wall of the execution chamber there is a quotation from a poem
by Ze'ev Jabotinsky, organizer of the Jewish battalion that fought with
the Allies in World War I, and founder of the Revisionist Party in
Zionism. His face decorates Israel's 1,000-pound bill. The poem was
written in response to those among the Jewish population who felt that
armed resistance against the British was unwise at best, criminal at
worst. Jabotinsky felt that "We have only one choice, to die or conquer
the mountain," as our ancestors did on Masada and in Betar.

Pay special attention to the photographs of Meyer Feinstein and
Moshe Barazani. Their cell can be seen on the left as you walk through
the museum. These men were quite young at the time of their condemnation, Barazani only seventeen and a half. The day before their
appointed execution, a hand grenade concealed in an orange was
smuggled into the prison for them. They used it to commit suicide
rather than submit to execution by the British. The shrapnel marks are
still visible in the wall of their cell. Read the official British disposition
papers on each case. The death sentence was imposed for "carrying
arms" and for "flogging British officers."

Leave the prison compound and turn right into the path behind
the Russian Church. Notice the row of low, cone-shaped pillars on your

right. These are tank-stoppers, nicknamed "Rommel's Teeth." Beyond, on the horizon, is the **Augusta Victoria Hospital** with its square Teutonic tower, and, to its left, the **Hebrew University** campus, both on Mount Scopus.

Leave the Russian Compound and turn left into **Helene Hamalka Street**. After about fifty yards you will reach the arched entranceway of No. 13. This is the **Agricultural Museum** founded by Moshe Dayan when he was Minister of Agriculture. The agricultural implements on view have been in use in Israel from time immemorial, and some of them can be seen in Arab and Bedouin villages today. The large, white stone wheel in the center of the first exhibit is an olive squasher. The olives are placed in the round groove at the bottom of the instrument and, when a man or animal pushes the wooden cross beam, the large stone wheel moves across the groove and cracks open the olives. The cracked olives are put into straw baskets, which are placed on the lower level of the large wooden instrument at the right of the stone wheel. The huge wooden screw turns the heavy beam down into the straw basket, crushing the olives further, and the oil seeps out below into the stone depression in front of the press. The olive residue in the basket isn't thrown out. It is a major source of fuel for heating village homes.

The water pumps just beyond are clever contraptions. Try to work them yourself so you can see how simply and efficiently they do their job. Notice the two hollowed stones lying in front of the largest pump. They are part of an ancient water conduit; the relief on the end of one fits hermetically into the groove on the end of the other. The large hole at the top makes for easier cleaning, much as does the modern manhole. Near the water pump there is a well and two round pieces of white marble, with grooves carved into them by the ropes which lowered and raised the buckets of water. From this spot, look out at the bordering Russian buildings. Each has a distinctive stone chimney with a pagoda-like construction on top.

The exhibit includes an ancient "morag," or flail, for threshing wheat. It looks like a large wooden abstract sculpture, but the black stones in the series of carved holes actually cut into the wheat kernels. The tool is usually activated by bouncing neighborhood children, or by a mule.

The exhibit is open only during office hours, and in the same compound you can also visit the offices of the **Society for the Protection of Nature**. They plan many hikes for nature lovers and they provide a

weekly schedule for the hardy and the less hardy. They will be happy
to advise which of their walks fit your particular constitution.

Are you tired? Then leave the Agricultural Museum, turn right,
walk to the end of Helene Hamalka Street and you will be once again
on Jaffa Road, where you can find the bus that brought you to Zion
Square.

If you would like to continue this walk to its termination, turn
right on **Yohanan Horqenos Street.** There is a fine little Chinese
restaurant on your left and a block away, on your right, is the
Hadassah-Seligsberg Vocational High School. The street becomes a
short flight of stairs and the narrow path at the top ends at **Harav Kook
Street.** A few steps toward the left will lead you to a recently restored
building with heavy black wrought iron decorations. This is **Maskit,**
where shopping is pure pleasure. Their collection of hand-made jewelry,
rugs, fabrics, children's and women's clothing is superb and made exclusively for Maskit, an organization that has developed a special program
for teaching primitive artisans how to produce for the modern market.
Its techniques have been adopted by many underdeveloped countries.
A good place for coffee and home-made cake is the little open courtyard in the back of the store.

When you leave the store turn right and walk to the intersection of
Hanevi'im Street, a street bordered on both sides by lovely old buildings. After all of your twists and turns you will scarcely realize that this
street is parallel to Jaffa Road.

Many of the buildings on this street are institutions that were
located as close as possible to the center of town and yet off the busy
main thoroughfare. At No. 58 you will see a particularly unusual structure built in 1882 by Conrad Schick, an architect and one of the first
modern historians of Jerusalem. The apartment in the gatehouse is still
in use.

At No. 54 there is a large open-air cafe, **Mifgash Bavli,** that serves
excellent vegetarian meals.

Turn right, as you leave the restaurant and walk a few steps to
Ethiopia Street, a short street built in the Turkish period. There are
many that consider this to be the most beautiful street in Jerusalem.
The homes are sited in a checkerboard pattern so that each has the
benefit of four exposures, four gardens and the illusion of complete
privacy on a sixteenth-of-an-acre lot. The checkerboard pattern can be
understood even without a site map when you notice that every other

building fronts on the street and every building in between is set far
back from the street. You must work up some courage and enter at
least one of the gardens that lies behind an iron gate. If your upbringing
does not allow such behavior you can peer into at least one garden
through some large holes conveniently cut into the iron gate by a fearful but thoughtful landowner.

The large circular building on your right is the **Ethiopian Church.**
The public may attend services at two in the afternoon, but the key-
keeper is a friendly gentleman who speaks a fine Hebrew; he may be
persuaded to let you in even at another hour. This church is Jerusalem's
only example of a "church-in-the-round," with the altar in the center,
following the form of the Holy of Holies in the Second Temple. Notice
the two Lions of Judah carved in the stone lintel above the entranceway; these are the symbols of Ethiopia, a reminder of its beginnings in
the union between the Queen of Sheba and King Solomon. Look for
the New Testament which is written entirely by hand on parchment, as
is the Old Testament in synagogues. There are also several hide-covered
drums, made according to ancient design, on which the priests play
during their Paschal (Passover) services.

Immediately opposite the church is the former home of **Eliezer Ben
Yehudah,** the stubborn man who, only 90 years ago, succeeded in
making Hebrew a modern spoken language. This is the first house in
Jerusalem in which this language was spoken daily in the family circle.
On the right of the door to the house you will see a rectangle of
chipped stone where the Municipality must periodically replace a
commemorative plaque after the right-wing Orthodox residents of
nearby areas pull it down. To these Jews, Ben Yehudah desecrated the
holiness of the Hebrew language which should be used only in study
and prayer. These people do not use it for everyday communication.
Instead, they speak Yiddish.

At the end of Ethiopia Street turn right into **Shelomo Zalman
Beharan Street,** named after the founder of **Me'a She'arim,** the community of ultra-Orthodox Jews which you will presently enter. The
houses you are passing are quite ordinary, each set on its own lot. This
is in marked contrast to the actual community of Me'a She'arim, which,
as you get closer, can be seen as one long house covering an entire
block. In fact, it is a series of row houses which cannot be entered from
the outside. The only access is through one of the gates spotted periodically around the circumference of the community. The founders of

Me'a She'arim had two reasons for constructing their community in this way. First, they really wanted to be a secluded community, where outside influences and a way of life contrary to their own would not intrude. Second, the community was built in the midst of utter desolation, and self-defense was a considerable factor in the form of development, which had to resemble as closely as economics would allow, a closed fortress. All closed or walled cities which can only be entered through barred gates are built with defense and protection foremost in mind, just as was the Old City of Jerusalem.

Incidentally, Me'a She'arim means "one hundred gates." A popular misconception holds that the name refers to the gates of the community itself, or to some grandiose scheme in the minds of the original developers. In fact, *me'a she'arim* is a phrase in the portion of the Bible read in the synagogue during that week in 1875 when the final decision to found a new community was taken. The phrase comes from the *Book of Genesis*: "Then Isaac sowed in that land and received in the same year a hundredfold (*me'a she'arim,*) and the Lord blessed him."

Turn right into **Rabbi Avraham Mislonim Street.** On some of the outer walls of Me'a She'arim you will see engraved stone tablets placed there in honor of residents of the Old City who purchased rooms in the new community for rental and who donated the proceeds to the community, which was supported solely by the good will of charitable persons. Most of the men in the community devote their entire lives to the study of Torah and they and their families receive a very small stipend from the community. Here education is the major industry. Once inside, a visit to any one of the numerous "cheders," (literally, "rooms," where boys learn their lessons) will give you a taste of the educational system once prevalent among East European Jews.

Turn into the gate on the left at No. 34. The gates were kept as narrow as possible so that the inhabitants could defend themselves against enemy intruders — as well as the local coyotes.

Although it looks like a narrow maze, the basic plan is so simple that, once inside, it is impossible to get lost. The community is shaped roughly like a rectangle, bound on all four sides by a row of buildings. The street you will be on when you enter the gate follows the rectangular row of houses. (The houses in the center of the rectangle were constructed later, when the community began to grow.) If you turn into this street, **Hevrat Shass Street,** you will be following the rectangle. Arrive on a Friday morning and you will see all the women-folk busily cleaning and scrubbing everything both inside and outside their tiny homes. You will see bearded men racing along the street, towels tucked under their arms, on the way to the ritual baths. And the people carrying something on a covered plate are undoubtedly bringing either the Sabbath *cholent* (a casserole of meat, beans and potatoes to be cooked for twenty-four hours and eaten after the synagogue service on Saturday morning) or unbaked Sabbath loaves to the public, community bakery. Follow the street as it turns to the right and then to the right again into the main commercial street of Me'a She'arim. Notice the covered wells on the stone-lined pavements to your right. The community now has running water but the wells were not destroyed because it is never known when the next emergency will arise. As long as its water supply is assured, a community can hold out indefinitely.

As you will see from the products offered for sale in the shops, the people who live here are poor. One vegetable shop actually sells only potatoes and green onions. The sign advertising the services of a letter writer is a holdover from the days when the community subsisted on the charitable contributions of rich men living abroad, whose continued support had to be periodically renewed through the mails. The **Me'a She'arim Yeshiva**, the main place of study and assembly, can be seen at the third opening to your right. Although it is the most influential institution in the community, it holds no monopoly over the religious lives of the inhabitants, who are encouraged to found small houses of study and worship of their own, as can be seen from the many synagogue entrances you have passed. To the left of the Yeshiva, there is a small, antique brass and copper-ware shop which you should enter. Those "in the know" come to this modest shop from far and near to purchase their home decorations. Mr. David Ezra, the proprietor, will let you know whether your selection is a genuine antique or merely a good reproduction.

Now, turn left to the vegetable market. Make another left turn and you will find yourself walking out the main gate of Me'a She'arim. Walk right on **Me'a She'arim Street** to look at the signs which express the community's opinions on various issues of the day. Many residents of the community are members of Neturai Kartah, a far-right-wing anti-Zionist group that believes only the Messiah can establish the State of Israel. Among other things, such as warnings against immodest dress and autopsies, their signs forbid their members to participate in national elections.

Walk into the **Free Kitchen** advertised on the right side of the street. Anyone who wishes may enter and have a free lunch of soup and bread, the mainstay of many people of this neighborhood during the week. Hopefully, you will probably never have another chance to see what a free kitchen is like. (Do remember to leave a donation.) If you prefer to avoid this experience, continue on your way till you get to the No. 11 bus stop sign. The bus will take you right back to Zion Square from where you started.

*Professional letter writers are still plying their trade
in Me'a She'arim*

THE SIXTH WALK

FROM DAMASCUS GATE THROUGH THE MOSLEM QUARTER

This walk will take you into the Old City: through passages on top of the Old City Wall; through the lanes and markets of the Moslem Quarter; to some of the northern defenses of the Old City as well as to the points at which these defenses were broken through in successive eras — by the Romans in the first century, the Crusaders in the eleventh, and by the Israeli Defense Forces in the twentieth century. The Old City is built, literally, in layers of stone, which themselves are the history of Jerusalem. The remains of one era provide the foundations for the next. Thus, the remnants of a Second-Temple pool built before the Common Era are the base for a Roman health center which itself rests beneath a Byzantine church. Above the Church, the Crusaders left their own mound of stones and on all sides there is a succession of Mameluke and Ottoman buildings. It takes only a few minutes to walk from a Turkish bath to the Via Dolorosa, with its symbols of Jesus' last agony.

Take this walk on any day but Sunday, when many of the churches on the Via Dolorosa are closed. Some close each day as well between 12 and 2. If you plan to do it on a Saturday or holiday, purchase tickets for Solomon's Quarry during the week at the Municipal Information Office on 34 Jaffa Street.

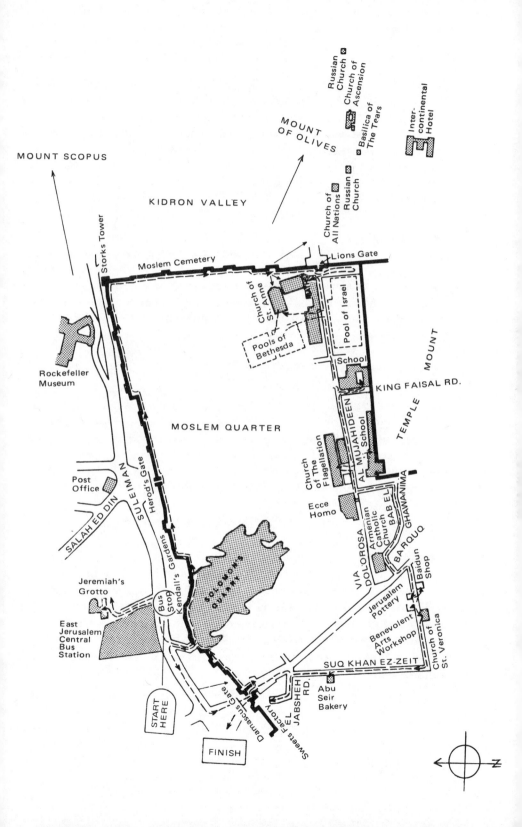

MOUNT SCOPUS

KIDRON VALLEY

MOUNT OF OLIVES

Russian Church
Church of Ascension
Basilica of The Tears
Inter-continental Hotel

Church of All Nations
Russian Church

Storks Tower

Moslem Cemetery

Lions Gate

Church of St. Anne

Pool of Israel

Pools of Bethesda

Rockefeller Museum

School

KING FAISAL RD.

TEMPLE MOUNT

MOSLEM QUARTER

AL MUJAHIDEEN School

Church of The Flagellation

Post Office

SALAH ED DIN

SULEIMAN

Herod's Gate

Ecce Homo

Armenian Catholic Church

BAB EL GHAWANIMA

BARQUQ

Baidun Shop

VIA DOLOROSA

Jeremiah's Grotto

Bus Stop

Kendall's Gardens

SOLOMON'S QUARRY

Jerusalem Pottery

Benevolent Arts Workshop

Church of St. Veronica

East Jerusalem Central Bus Station

SUQ KHAN EZ-ZEIT

START HERE

EL JABSHEH RD.

Damascus Gate

Sweets Factory

Abu Seir Bakery

FINISH

N

Take the No. 12 bus from West Jerusalem to the **Damascus Gate** stop. Directly in front of you is the North Wall of the Old City, built at this point upon a rock outcrop. (At night, it is illuminated to show the rock veins to best advantage.) The outcrop is part of a huge vein that once covered this northern area of the city. The main street was dug directly through the rock bed, forming a moatlike buffer zone around the wall, for the city rises again on its rock bed on the other side of the street. The street is named for Suleiman the Magnificent, the Sultan who built the wall and its gates in the first half of the sixteenth century on the remains of far earlier walls. Beneath the Sultan's Wall lie the walls of Jerusalem that were built by the Romans and those that were built later by the Crusaders. Every conqueror of Jerusalem breached the walls built by his predecessor, rebuilt the walls he had broken which were breached again by the next conqueror. Legend has it that the Sultan's wife inspired the construction of his wall. In fact, the undertaking was financed by an Egyptian Jew named DeCastro.

Cross the street, on the zebra lines of the nearest crosswalk, turn right, and soon you will come to a nameless alleyway bordering the **Central Bus Station** on its right side. To make sure you have found the correct alleyway, look for a sign at its entrance announcing "Bob's Snack Shop." At the far end of the alleyway, you can see a large outcropping of rock on the facing wall. This is the continuation of the vein you just saw at the base of the Old City Wall. Obviously, two such outcroppings around the city wall double the work of an invader who must first descend into the street and then climb up again if he is to reach and breach the Old City Wall.

At the end of the alleyway there is a small mosque, and in its outer yard there is a large pile of clay pots offered for sale by the keeper of the mosque. Different kinds of pots are produced in different sections of the country; the urn-shaped pots of red are from Hebron, the black ones and the painted ones from the Gaza Strip. If it is prayer time, you will see a line of shoes outside the mosque as well as a stack of extra straw kneeling pads. There is no minaret on this mosque; a simple loudspeaker does well enough to call the faithful to prayer.

Walk into the **Assalam Pananis Store** next door to the mosque. This banana warehouse is delightfully cool and it may take a moment to realize that you are really in an ancient stone quarry. Pilgrims of the Middle Ages mentioned it in letters home as **Jeremiah's Grotto** on the notion that it was here that the prophet was imprisoned by King

Zedekiah for prophesying the destruction of Jerusalem by the Babylonians. There is no evidence that this cave is in fact the cave mentioned in the Bible where this event took place, but tradition dies
hard, and Jeremiah's Grotto it remains. The stone quarried here is
called royal stone, for it provided the building blocks of King Herod's
great Jerusalem. It is a soft stone, easy to remove with primitive instruments and lending itself readily to the chisel of the Arab stone dresser.
The harder stone, used to build most of West Jerusalem, is called Jew
stone. It can be quarried only with modern tools and is extremely
difficult to dress by hand. Finding even the small amount of royal
stone needed to repair wartime damage to the Old City was a serious
municipal problem after the Six-Day War.

Cross the street and return to the Old City Wall. Look up at the
building protruding above the wall line from inside the City. A row of
triangles lines the topmost level of the building. The open round spaces
of which each triangle is composed are made of clay pipes. They lead
cool air onto the enclosed balconies and a bit of water placed in the
pipes in the early morning will keep the balcony cool throughout the
day.

Walk to your right on the sidewalk parallel to the wall. Soon you
will come to a gate in the wrought-iron fence leading into **Kendall's
Gardens**, which were planned and executed by the last British town
planner of Jerusalem as part of a city beautification program.

The garden path on your right will take you to **Solomon's Quarry**.
It is open from 8 to 6 daily. Tickets for a Saturday or holiday visit
must be purchased at the Municipal Information Office at 34 Jaffa
Road. This huge series of caves lies directly beneath the Old City and
supports the houses and streets of the Moslem Quarter. It supplied the
building stones for ancient Jerusalem. Although it was known that such
a quarry existed under the Old City, its entrance had been lost for
centuries and was only rediscovered by chance some hundred years ago
when a Jerusalem gentleman, taking his moning stroll, was led to the
opening by the sniffing of his dog. He kept his discovery secret, fearful
lest the Turkish régime mishandle the matter, and returned later to
make a thorough investigation by torchlight. (The electric torches that
mark the safe path you follow today were, of course, not available to
him.) To keep from getting lost in the labyrinth, he tied a string to a
stalagmite at the entrance and unraveled it as he made his way through.
It **was** the British Mandatory government that opened the caves to the

Solomon's Quarries by torchlight

public and Jerusalemites still remember exploring the caves with only a fiery torch to guide them.

Look carefully at the wall on your right to see the marks made by the primitive tools used in cutting huge blocks of stone, some of them weighing up to 100 tons.

The largest open space in the series of caves is called the **Masons' Hall**. The masons, who consider themselves the ideological descendants of the people of the Second Temple, held their international meetings here until 1948, when the City was split in two.

As you walk deeper into the caves you will hear the dripping of water. At one spot, water has seeped in in sufficient quantity to form a small pool. This run-off water is seeping in from the Old City above, but, according to legend, it is the tears of King Zedekiah, he who imprisoned Jeremiah the Prophet in the quarry to the north. It is told that he tried to escape from the conquering Babylonians (Jeremiah's prophecy did come true) through this subterranean passage. However, at the same moment, a gazelle was racing above ground trying to escape the Babylonian king's hunt. When Zedekiah emerged from the cave, both he and the gazelle were captured. Zedekiah's sons, the heirs to the throne of Judah, were put to death before his eyes, and immediately after, he himself was blinded so that the death of his sons should remain forever as his last sight.

Keep going, even though the atmosphere is eerie. It is impossible to get lost here; the lighted path takes you right back to the entrance.

When you leave Solomon's Quarry, walk through the iron gate and turn to your left. As you walk toward Damascus Gate, the **Convent of Notre Dame de Paris** will be on the horizon, marked by a statue on the roof of the long, arcaded building. Until the Six-Day War its rooftop observation point was the best place for West Jerusalemites to get a good look at the Old City.

Continue on to Damascus Gate, the largest and most impressive in the City Wall. Through the centuries, it has been known by a number of names: *Sha'ar Shechem* in Hebrew, because the road leading out of the gate connects Jerusalem with the city of Shechem (Nablus); *Porta Neapolis* by the Romans, who gave that name to Shechem; *Bab el Amud* in Arabic, after a stone pillar for marking distances that once stood in the mouth of the gate. (A stone pillar is sited at this location on the fourth-century Madeba Map, a reproduction of which you saw in the floor of the Y.M.C.A. on the Fourth Walk.)

The road outside the gate is a good twenty-five feet higher than the entrance to the City at the gate itself. The depression marks the beginning of the **Tyropoeon, or Cheesemaker's Valley,** which runs through the entire city, emerging at the southern end to form one of the boundaries of the "City of David," the original Biblical Jerusalem.

Although the valley is barely discernible today, it gave form to Second-Temple Jerusalem, dividing the City into two parts that were connected by valley-spanning bridges.

The gate is an excellent example of Ottoman architecture, with its Saracen decorative motifs, rigid crenelated towers, machicolations, or stone boxes used to protect the defenders of the towers, and gun- (or arrow-) slits. As you walk down the circular staircase leading to the gate, look over the rim of the stone wall to the deep depression below the gate. This is an excellent place from which to see the layers of the City. The stones at the base of the wall are typical Herodian masonry, large blocks, carefully dressed, with an indented margin carved on all four sides, King Herod's "signature." (His name crops up frequently on these walks, for under his reign, from 64-4 B.C., the final version of the Second Temple was erected and Jerusalem reached its zenith as the City Beautiful.) No mortar was needed to hold these stones together — that job is done by the weight of the stones and their adjustment to one another, which is so close that even a knife cannot be wedged between them.

The blocked-up archway with broken pillar bases on either side is the gate to the City which the Romans built when they destroyed Herod's Jerusalem and constructed Aelia Capitolina on and with its remains. The Roman period lasted from 70 — 324 A.D. If you look carefully at the lintel above the keystone of the arched gateway, you can make out the letters C A P , part of the engraved tablet announcing that this is Aelia C A Pitolina.

It was the Romans who established the boundaries of Jerusalem that we now see encircled by Suleiman's stone wall. The Romans built it according to the standard plan for a Roman Empire garrison town. Each side of the almost square wall was one kilometer long (a bit less than two-thirds of a mile). Each side was pierced in the center by a large gate. The main roads of the city started at each of the four gates and met in the center of the town. Each road was lined with pillars, which accounts for the pillar bases on either side of the gateway. The two road axes divided the city into four quarters. This is the origin of the four quarters of Jerusalem today: the Jewish, the Christian, the Armenian and the Moslem. You will see the original North-South Roman road on your eighth walk, in the Jewish Quarter.

The Roman gate was discovered only a few decades ago in the course of an archaeological dig at its base. In front of this gateway and a little to your right is a pile of stone, the remains of the **Church of St. Abraham**, a Crusader structure that was also lost until the dig that removed the rubble of successive destructions.

Rest awhile on the ledge of the staircase and watch the parade of people marching in and out of the gate. The women in long black embroidered dresses are *fellahin* (peasants), probably coming to the big city to sell the produce of their villages. Anyone wearing a green turban has been on a pilgrimage to Mecca. The turbaned priests are Egyptians of the Coptic Church, and the clergymen with tall, flowing headress are of the Armenian Church. If a vendor is nearby, buy a sesame roll and eat bits of it dipped into the pinch of spices wrapped in newspaper which is supplied free of charge on request.

After your rest, enter the gatehouse itself, which is built in the zig-zag shape characteristic of all the city's gates. The purpose of this floor plan is to give the defenders of the city a second and third chance to get at the enemy invader should he succeed in breaching the gate. Since the enemy holds his shield in the left hand, he will always be presenting his unprotected side to the defenders as he makes his way through the turns in the gatehouse.

When you leave the gatehouse, turn to the left and, at the first opportunity, to the left again. There is a staircase here; follow it to a second staircase — very narrow — on your left fronted by a gray iron door. At the top of this staircase you will see one of the gunslits that you saw from below. Look through it, as might a defender of the tower, to see the enemy below. (This is a very smelly place, but do not be discouraged: the rest of this walk is neat and clean.) Follow the staircase through another iron gate. You are now standing on the very roof of the gatehouse. The bumps on the roof are the vaults of the ceiling below.

Look out over the cityscape within the wall. Most of the houses, even the crudest, are domed; this is the least expensive way to span space in areas where wooden beams are scarce.

A staircase leads up to a narrow ledge forming a semicircle off to your left.

Stand on the far end of the semicircle and look down into the main street leading from Damascus Gate into the City. This is the Tyropoeon Valley, the beginnings of which you saw outside the gate. You can follow it through the entire length of the City until it emerges at the South Wall in a V-shaped depression almost at the edge of the horizon directly opposite your observation point.

The barren hills on the horizon are part of the Judean Desert. It was this valley line that the Romans used as the basis for the major road of Aelia Capitolina. The valley line now divides the city into the Christian Quarter lying on your right, and the Moslem Quarter on your left, the latter distinguished by the golden dome of the Mosque, the former by the two domes of the Church of the Holy Sepulchre. A sharp eye can spot the Jewish Cemetery on the Mount of Olives, lying, visually, between the golden dome and the minaret rising to its left. Beyond is the Jerusalem Intercontinental Hotel, a lodestar on the Jerusalem horizon.

You are now standing on the fourth level of the gatehouse. Walk back down to the third level and turn left. Here the rampart walk begins. From it, you can look directly down into the Moslem Quarter of the Old City and, by merely peering through the crenelations, into the City outside the wall. Notice that, at some places, the land within the City reaches almost to the top of the wall; this is the effect of centuries of accumulated rubble that was poured here until the ground level of the City rose higher and higher. Some patches of ground around the buildings bordering the wall are used for gardening. A nature lover should be able to distinguish among the carob, pine, palm, acacia, oleander and fig trees.

Soon you will be able to look through the crenelations at the Central Bus Station outside the wall and at the rock vein you saw outside Jeremiah's Grotto. From this vantage point, the position of the street as a defensive buffer is especially clear.

If you were walking through the Moslem Quarter at ground level you would never suspect that it contained so many parks and playgrounds.

A set of iron stairs leads you to the roof of **Herod's Gate**, which leads directly into the heart of the Moslem Quarter. From the roof of the gate you can make out the four towers that punctuate the Mount Scopus-Mount of Olives horizon. You have seen them often from different places within the City. The one directly in front of you, shorter and squatter than the others, is the tower of **Augusta Victoria Hospital**, on the lower slope of Mount Scopus. The one to your immediate right and the tallest of the four is the tower of the Russian church in the Arab village of **E-Tur** on the Mount of Olives. The smaller one, shaped like a minaret, marks the **Church of Ascension**, where, according to tradition, Jesus rose up to heaven. The church grounds also house a mosque, thus a minaret on one of the holiest sites in Christendom. On the far left is the tower of the **Hebrew University** on Mount Scopus.

Descend another iron staircase leading from the gatehouse roof back to the rampart walk. A sign points the way to **St. Stephen's Gate**. (Occasionally, soldiers are posted on the roof of Herod's gatehouse with orders to stop anyone from continuing on the rampart walk. Naturally, you must obey them and walk down the stairs of the gatehouse to find St. Stephen's Gate from ground level. This is not so difficult: just keep to the east and ask for directions).

From your position above the Moslem Quarter, a number of things come to view that are not apparent on street level. First, the large amount of open space which is devoted to vegetable farming. Onions, grapes, peaches, artichokes and gooseberries are grown for market within the densely populated city. Second, note that the tightly packed houses you see from the street are built in groupings that surround an open courtyard. This is a form widely used in Mediterranean countries, where the courtyard serves as community center — even for the family livestock.

Notice the huge wall of cactus which acts as a property divider — certainly more effective than the rusty tin cans you see elsewhere used for the same purpose.

Approaching the **Rockefeller Museum,** which lies opposite the northeast corner of the wall, you will notice large pockmarks on the squat, turreted tower in the center of the golden-stoned building. The museum, which contains a priceless collection of antiquities, suffered extensive shelling during the Six-Day War. Many died fighting in its formal English gardens.

In 1099 when Godfrey de Bouillon conquered Jerusalem, his camp of Crusader warriors was set up in what is now the garden of the museum and it was the portion of the Wall opposite the garden that was breached to enter the walled City. What today is the Moslem Quarter, was then the Jewish Quarter, and the Jews, huddled in their synagogue which lay in the path of the victorious Crusaders, were the first Jerusalemites to be massacred. The Romans, too, made their successful entry into the City from this northern point. The tall pine you see in the museum garden is one of the most ancient trees in Jerusalem. It appears that this tree has acquired immunity against weaponry, but, in the great snowfall of 1968, it suffered mightily.

The rectangular **Storks Tower** forms the northeast corner of the wall. Look down from its eastern side. Directly beneath you is a **Moslem cemetery.** At its edge, you will see a monument larger than all the others. This is a memorial erected by the Arab community to its fallen after the Six-Day War.

From the southern edge of the Storks Tower you will see a large open space directly below. If it is Friday morning, an animal fair will be in progress, the sellers noisily pleading the virtues of their sheep and donkeys, the buyers suspiciously examining each and every portion of the goods.

The **Kidron Valley** runs parallel to the wall along its entire eastern length. At one time, the valley came as close to the wall as does
the Valley of Hinnom, which you saw on the western side of the
Old City. A sharp "glacis" once rose from the valley to the wall,
but it has been obliterated by the age-old practice of using the
Kidron as a municipal dumping ground. Centuries of debris lie beneath the level ground between the line of the valley today and the
wall.

Walk down from the Storks Tower via an enclosed narrow staircase and turn to your left. You have now left the north wall and
are walking on the east wall of the Old City. A word of warning:
stay away from the gray-green weeds whose stems are covered with
round balls the size of marbles. These are stinging nettles and
exposure to them can cause you as much grief as exposure to poi-
son ivy.

The Moslem cemetery continues almost the entire length of the
east wall. Notice the long, low oblong graves. These are mass burial
places, either for the poor or for victims of massacres. It is assumed
that the southern end of this cemetery was built upon the remains of
the Second Temple; it is known that after the destruction the Romans
had to clear the Temple Mount of rubble before they could build
their own temples to the gods, and the only dumping ground available
was the Kidron Valley.

Anywhere along this stretch of the walk you may be approached
by a gentleman claiming to be the keeper of the wall. He may demand
payment for permission to continue this walk, but he is entirely self-
appointed and no fee is due him.

As you approach the **Lions Gate**, (or **St. Stephen's Gate**) which
marks the end of the rampart walk, look out over the Old City. The
buildings seem to rise up in layers around a low-lying area which, in the
days of the Second Temple, was a large pool, the **Bethesda**. In the foreground is the upper portion of the **Church of St. Anne** which is shaped
in the form of a cross, with a low dome rising at the point where the
axes of the cross meet. You will get a different view of both the Church
and the Pool, with its famed archaeological dig, when your walk reaches
street level.

When you reach the very last bastion of the wall before the Lions
Gate, look out over the Mount of Olives rising beyond the Kidron
Valley to see the **Church of Gethsemane** with a brightly colored mosaic

triangle above the entrance pillars; behind it, the many onion domes of the **Russian Church,** and behind that, the black and white **Basilica of the Tears,** said to be the place where Christ looked down upon Jerusalem on his last pilgrimage, and wept when he foresaw the imminent destruction of the City. If you look a little father south, you can see the gravestones of the **Mount of Olives Jewish Cemetery** rising up to the borders of the **Intercontinental Hotel.** The *Book of Joel* states that the Last Judgment will take place in the Kidron Valley. It was therefore assumed that the pious should be buried close enough to the scene so that their bodies would not have to roll great distances to reach the spot on the Mighty Day. A legend holds that when the Day arrives two bridges will be constructed spanning the valley from the Mount of Olives to the Temple Mount. The righteous will walk safely on one; the evil will fall from the other to eternal damnation in the valley below.

From this spot you have a low-flying bird's eye view of the **Temple Mount.** You can easily spot its three major landmarks: the silver dome of the **El Aqsa Mosque,** the golden **Dome of the Rock,** and the smallest, the **Dome of the Chain,** lying between the other two.

The Temple Mount is actually a gigantic land-fill operation undertaken by King Herod to provide a suitable foundation for the Second Temple. The site was on Mount Moriah, where the First Temple had been built by King Solomon. King Herod built huge retaining walls around the hill, some of them as high as 144 feet. The eastern and southern retaining walls of the Temple Mount are part of the Wall of the Old City. The western retaining wall is the famed Western Wall. The northern retaining wall can be seen clearly from the roof of the Lions Gate, just a few yards ahead on the rampart walk. A large building was constructed on top of the retaining wall but some of the huge Herodian stones that lie beneath can still be seen. The Herodian wall itself, of course, descends far below the surface you now see. The huge open space in front of this northern boundary of the Temple Mount was a large pool, in existence since the days of the Second Temple. Called the **Pool of Israel,** it was filled in and paved by the British Government in the 1930's at the request of the Grand Mufti of Jerusalem, who wanted to rid the Old City of the name Israel. Sitting in the center of the pool area is a barrack trimmed in blue. This is a **United Nations Relief Station** where Arabs with U.N. ration cards can receive oil and flour.

Before you is **Al-Mujahideen Road.** (You can easily see the street sign from your position on high.) Some traditions hold that nearby, on a street parallel to this road, Jesus was brought by the Roman soldiers from Gethsemane to be judged at the **Fortress of Antonia**, which once marked the northwest corner of the Temple Mount.

Notice the six-pointed star motif decorating the southern face of the gatehouse. It appears that some symbols have beneficent connotations for more than one group of people.

Leave the rampart walk via the staircase at the Temple Mount Wall. You have been walking above the route taken by observant Jews on the fast day of Tisha B'Av, which memorializes the destruction of the First and Second Temples. For it is commanded in *Psalms:* "Walk about Zion, go round about her, count her towers, consider well her ramparts, go through her citadels."

Walk through the gatehouse to look at the front face of the **Lions Gate**. It is also known as **St. Stephen's Gate**, for it is said that the first Christian martyr was led through this gate to be stoned to death in the Kidron Valley. It was through this gate that the Israeli Army broke into the Old City during the 1967 War and reached the Western Wall. Tough paratroopers were seen weeping at the sight of that ancient wall, which had been closed off to Jews by the Jordanians for 19 years. Wartime damage to the gate has been repaired; the older stones are easily distinguished from the replacements. In time the new stones will also acquire a dark patina so that some future archaeologist may have difficulty dating the gate. It is just such repair work in the past that clouds the facts about a number of ancient remains in the city. The huge doors in the gateway are reproductions, but they hold true to original form in their long strips of iron held together by huge iron nails.

There is a legend that Sultan Suleiman built the Wall and its gates after a dreadful nightmare which warned that unless he did so he would be destroyed at the hands of lions. To attest to the successful completion of his night-time commandment he instructed that lions adorn this gate, the last in the wall's circuit.

You have reached the midway point in the Sixth Walk. If you prefer to continue this walk tomorrow, walk away from the Walls to the main road where you will be able to flag a cab or hop an Arab bus to Damascus Gate. You will not be able to find any other transportation until the end of this walk.

To continue the walk.....The Lions Gate was originally built in the traditional zigzag form, with its exit on the left. The advent of vehicular traffic made it necessary to cut a direct opening in the gatehouse.

Walk through this new opening. On the right-hand corner of Al-Mujahideen Road, you will see a large arch with an Arabic inscription. This
was once a sebil, or watering place. Sultan Suleiman built many sebils
in Jerusalem — most of them more elegant than this rather poor example — to serve the needs of travelers and pilgrims. When the local populace took to using the sebil as a public lavatory, it was stoned in and, as
you see, now forms the wall of a building that was built still later. This
phenomenon is quite common in Old Jerusalem, where you can often
see a bricked-in arch forming part of the wall of a newer building:
another example of the way in which a city is built in layers, the lower
level becoming an integral part of the upper.

Turn to your right for a visit to the **Turkish Baths.** A Turkish Bath
may be defined as a highly ritualized form of social intercourse, and
while this bathhouse is not the most gracious example, it does follow
the traditional form. The hottest room is called the *caldarium*. Hot
water is cooked up someplace adjacent to the room and flows through
the pipes beneath the stone floor. So that not a vapor can escape, the
room is windowless, light coming in through glassed-in holes in the
roof. The next room is middling-hot, offering an opportunity to
recuperate slowly from the effects of the steam; this is the *tepidarium*.
Next, one should enter a narrow passageway where the air itself seems
to have been frozen — known, quite aptly, as the *frigidarium*, but this
bathhouse has "lost its cool." Finally, there is a room with lounging
benches lining all the walls (a typical Arab living room is furnished in
the same way) where the bathers can relax and gossip with their neighbors before returning to real life. This is the *apoditorium*. In the center
of the room, there is a traditional water fountain with a Greek name —
kantharos — this one said to be five hundred years old.

Continue on Al-Mujahideen Road to **Sainte Anne's Church.** A bulletin board to the right of the entrance announces that this church was
built upon the birthplace of the Virgin Mary and that within its
boundaries once lay the **Piscine de** (Pool of) **Bethesda.** There is also a
site plan which attempts to show the relationship between what you
can now see and what was once on the ground. The gardens contain dis-
plays of carved capitals and decorated lintels that were found during
the course of explorations of the church grounds.

Follow the stone pathway to the main entrance of the church,
which was built by the Crusaders in the twelfth century. At that time,
European architecture was in the process of transition between Roman-

esque and Gothic, and the church reflects some elements of both styles. When Saladin wrested control of the city from the Crusaders in 1187, he converted the church into a Moslem theological seminary, which accounts for the Arabic inscription above the entrance. It was subsequently used as a stable. Not until the nineteenth century, 700 years after its construction, was any major restoration work undertaken. Built on the classic European plan, the long central section, or nave, is taller than the two side wings, which form the interior side aisles and balconies. The facade of each wing contains one window; when the sun is reaching its noon-time zenith, rays of light enter the church and form a path leading to the central altar in the apse behind the transept. The classic pattern of the cross, formed by the axis of the nave and the axis of the transept, will be clear when you enter the church. The interior is pure form, completely bare of decoration. The most ancient item in the building is the stone lintel above the side entrance to the church, which bears a Byzantine cross encircled by a wreath.

Some of the residents of the Moslem Quarter found refuge in this church during the Six-Day War and sent the White Fathers (Jesuits) to the Israeli soldiers with their plea for surrender.

Leave the church and turn right. Before you reach the site of the archaeological dig, you will see a tablet leaning against a stone fence. The tablet was found on the site. Its Greek letters tell about a man named Amos and a pool named Probatica (the Greek name for the Pool of Bethesda). The last letter on the third line is "pi," the first letter on the fourth line "rho," and the subsequent letters clearly finish the name.

The area was excavated in the 1950's by Père Benoit, who uncovered four different levels of construction. The lowest level is the pool itself, dating from the time of the Second Temple. A look at the sides of the excavation site will show you the sheer rock face of the pool. It covered a much more extensive area than does the dig. The pool was divided in half by a bridge, which is the highest level of the dig and runs east and west in a relatively narrow ridge down the middle of the excavation site. The waters on one side were used for cleansing sacrificial sheep and the other for human ritual baths. This is the pool mentioned in the New Testament: "Now there is in Jerusalem by the sheep gate a pool, in Hebrew called Beth-za'tha, which has five porticoes. In these lay a multitude of invalids, blind, lame, paralyzed. One man was there who had been ill for thirty-eight years. When Jesus saw him...he said, 'Do you want to be healed?' The sick man answered him, 'Sir, I have no man to put me into the pool...and while I am going another steps down before me.' Jesus said to him, 'Rise, take up your pallet, and walk.' And at once the man was healed."

The Romans, next in line of succession, were heirs to the tradition of healing waters, and conducted a health center here. An ample supply of votives to the Roman God of Healing Aesculapius and his daughter Hygeia were found on the site, each marked with the caduceus, the classic symbol of medicine: a serpent wound around a staff. Coins from Roman Jerusalem are marked with the same sign, as were all coins used in cities where the Romans maintained a health center. (Bethesda, Maryland, the site of the U.S. Army Hospital, carries on this tradition.) There is an old legend that an angel flies over this pool once every twenty-four hours and whoever happens to be in the pool at the time is miraculously cured.

When the Byzantines succeeded the Romans in 324 A.D., they constructed a church on the site of the pool. Since the bridge was too narrow to support an entire church structure they used it only for the nave, and the side aisles were built directly above the pool and supported by huge arches. One of them can be seen almost in its entirety descending to the bottom of the pool. The four pillar bases in the center of the bridge once supported the roof of the nave. The Byzantine crosses on the bases can be clearly seen and one pillar is in perfect condition where it was found *in situ*, a Latin term used by archaeologists to describe anything found in the exact position in which it was constructed.

Don't be afraid to climb in and out among the levels; if you make no foolhardy leaps, it is really quite safe and a wonderful adventure.

Leave the church grounds and continue to walk on Al-Mujahideen Road. The rooms built above the street and attached to the buildings on either side are typical of the Old City, providing shade to pedestrians as well as extra living space.

On the right side of the road, just before you reach the intersection of Al-Mujahideen and King Faisal Roads, there is an entrance into a typical courtyard such as those you saw from above on the rampart walk. A lemon tree and a huge stone ceiling provide shade for the families and their collection of caged doves.

Turn left into **King Faisal Road**. At the end of the short road, marked by another opening onto the Temple Mount, turn into the gate on your right to see a fine example of a Mameluke building used as a schoolhouse. As you return to Al-Mujahideen Road you will see a barred opening in the wall bordering the street. It looks into a small cemetery where important community personages lie buried under the branches of a spreading fig tree.

Continue on Al-Mujahideen Road until you can see a series of domes on the right. On your left there is a long, low-slung staircase leading up to the **El Umariyah School.** A sign above the entrance states in Hebrew and Arabic that this is a government school for boys. Walk into the large interior courtyard. Every Friday afternoon at three o'clock the Franciscan Fathers gather here to begin their weekly procession to the Stations of the Cross, for they believe that here was the First Station. It is known that this courtyard was part of the Antonio Fortress which contained the Praetorium, where in the *Gospel According to John,* Pontius Pilate conducted the judgment of Jesus. In 70 A.D., when the Romans broke into the city through the North Wall, they made their way to the Antonia Fortress. This was Jerusalem's last stronghold and it had to be conquered before the Roman Army could continue on to take the Temple Mount. Josephus Flavius, the historian of the period and a contemporary of the events described, writes about the Fortress: "Now on the north side of the temple was built a citadel, whose walls were square and strong and of extraordinary firmness... But for the tower itself, when Herod the King of the Jews had fortified it more firmly than before, in order to secure and guard the temple, he gratified Antonius, who was his friend...and then gave it the name of the Tower of Antonia." Mark Antony had been instrumental in securing the kingship for Herod and had also protected the king from his enemy Cleopatra.

Walk up to the second level of the courtyard and look through the barred window onto the Temple Mount. Ever since the destruction of the Second Temple, Jewish religious law has forbidden the pious to enter the Temple Mount, lest they tread on what may have been the Holy of Holies. They had to be content with a view from a barred window.

If you have the energy and want a really spectacular view of the Temple Mount, go up one more level via the staircase on your left. The hills in the distance beyond the Temple Mount are the Hills of Moab in Jordan. From this spot you can look out again over the Old City as you did from atop Damascus Gate, but now the view is in reverse. Here, too, the Tyropoeon Valley running through the length of the city can be comprehended rather than actually seen, for the buildings appear to slope downward into the valley depression. Now, look over to the Moslem Quarter of the Old City. In front of you are two buildings which you will soon enter — the **Church of the Flagellation** and the **Chapel of Ecce Homo**. From this exterior view you can see the complex arrangement of intricately related wings and arcades, patterns which will not be immediately apparent from down below.

When you leave the school, turn to your right and walk some twenty paces to the Church of the Flagellation. To the right of the main entrance there is an inscription from the *Gospel According to John*: "Then Pilate took Jesus and scourged him. And the soldiers plaited a crown of thorns, and put it on his head." The long, low building facing the entrance to the churchyard is a Franciscan theological seminary, the chapel on your right commemorates the flagellation, and the church itself on your left, Jesus' taking on of the cross. Just outside the door of the church is a site plan which shows the relationship of this complex to the Herodian complex. The stones of the floor inside the church, once part of the inner courtyard of the Tower of Antonia, are striated to keep the Roman soldiers' horses from slipping.

Leave the Flagellation compound and turn right. At the next building, the Convent de Ecce Homo, Al-Mujahideen Road ends and the **Via Dolorosa** begins. Notice that just beyond the entrance to the convent there is an arched buttress leading from the opposite side of the street directly into the building. It plays an important role in the history of the convent.

You will find cold drinks in the entrance — one of the first signs of the gracious solicitude which the Sisters extend to all visitors. The primary mission of the Sisters of Zion is to teach pilgrims and residents of all faiths about the history of Jerusalem, its archaeology and topography. Their monthly bulletin is called the *Zionist Copybook*, and on the second floor of the convent they conduct an *ulpan* where Jews may learn Arabic and Arabs, Hebrew. The Sisters of Zion are the feminine branch of the Fathers of Zion, an order founded by the Ratisbonne Brothers, who converted to Christianity in the early part of the 1800's. The older brother founded the order in thanksgiving for the conversion of his younger brother. Its purpose then as now was ecumenical, the promotion of mutual understanding among all religions. The younger brother thought as did others at the time, that the arch he saw outside

*The Ecce Homo Arch
on the Via Dolorosa.
Except for the shoeless
pedestrian, it might as
well be today*

the building was the arch of Ecce Homo, where Pilate said to the waiting multitudes, "Here is the man," in Latin, Ecce Homo. He did not realize that the arch was second-century Roman and thus could not have been in existence when Jesus was condemned.

You will not be allowed to tour the building by yourself. The Sisters themselves conduct visitors through and have set up classrooms with visual aids to assist in the learning process. Under their expert guidance you will see the continuation of the Ecce Homo Arch (actually, Emperor Hadrian's triumphal arch), the magnificent **Double Pool** which provided water for the Antonia Fortress, the Herodian pavement of the **Lithostrothos** where Roman soldiers carved games in the stones to wile away the hours of their guard duty.

When you leave the convent, walk a few paces to your left, and turn into **Bab el-Ghawanima Street.** It will lead you down some broad steps under a vaulted covering. At the bottom of the road you will see another entranceway into the Temple Mount. All roads in the Moslem Quarter lead to the Temple Mount.

Take the staircase on your right to a narrow lane typical of the Moslem Quarter, one that opens suddenly onto a splendid cityscape. Notice the concrete inserts on the stone treads. These enable carts to navigate the streets more easily. The staircase suddenly becomes **Barquq Road.** Before you is the dome of the **Armenian Catholic Church,** the Third Station on the Via Dolorosa. (At the end of the staircase you will once again be on Via Dolorosa.) Turn left, then right at the Fifth Station of the Cross. A stone tablet at the Station shows two arms outstretched, one bare, the other clothed. The bare arm is Jesus' and the clothed that of St. Francis of Assisi. Both bear the marks of the Cross. The Franciscan Cross, above, represents the body of Christ and the four wounds made by the Cross.

All along this stretch of the Via Dolorosa you will see small shops with excellent collections of antiquities. Don't buy anything unless you are with someone who knows about such things; any wise antiquity merchant can spot a novice from a distance of 100 meters. The **Baidun Shop** on your left is the most interesting of its kind and should be looked into. The owner knows his antiquities well and if you look as though you are ready to make a purchase, he will offer you some excellent minted tea or Turkish coffee. If you select silver jewelry you will be charged by weight and not necessarily by workmanship. A bit further up the street and on your right is the **Jerusalem Pottery Shop** where an Armenian family has been producing lovely middle-eastern designs on enamel for generations. Next door is the **Benevolent Arts Workshop** where dresses and tablecloths trimmed with fine Arab hand embroidery are made to order. Prices are fixed and relatively reasonable; the shop is actually a training center for young Arab women who work as apprentice embroiderers.

Walk into the **Sixth Station of the Cross** on your left where, it is believed, St. Veronica stepped out of her home to wipe Jesus' brow as he labored under the Cross. To the right of the main chapel a staircase leads down to an underground cavern converted into a chapel. Many buildings in this Quarter lead similarly hidden lives. The last four stations of the Cross are in the **Church of the Holy Sepulchre** which you will visit on the next walk.

Via Dolorosa continues as a staircase under a series of arches. Staired streets are commonly used to scale differences in topography.

At the top of the stairs you come to **Suq Khan Ez-Zeit**, the Olive Oil Market. Leading off to your left is the famous covered markets where specialized products are sold — the Spice Market, the Goldsmith Market and the Meat Market. You will have an opportunity to visit them on your Eighth Walk, but now, turn to your right. There are a number of unusual things to sample as you walk through this market. The honeyed nuts sold by street vendors are very nice. Walk into any one of the nut shops and sample some of the unfamiliar varieties, such as dried chickpeas and roasted watermelon seeds. The candy shops specialize in Turkish Delight and pressed apricot "leather." Walk into the **Abou Seir Bakery**, on your left at No. 22, for some excellent baklava and eat it right there with Turkish coffee or mint tea.

Notice that all the nations of the world seem to have gathered in this market place, earlocked Jews, Ethiopian priests, Arab women weighing their goods on primitive hand scales, Greek and Russian clergymen, their hair gathered behind in a knot, not to mention the multitude of tourist and local bargain-hunters.

At the end of the market, turn left into **El Jabsheh Road**. At the very top, you will find a candy factory where the sweets you have just tasted are manufactured. Ask the owners to show you around.

Walk back down El Jabsheh Road. You are now on the street leading directly into **Damascus Gate**. As you walk to the gate, notice the cafes on your right where men spend a good deal of their leisure time smoking nargilehs (water pipes) and playing sheshbesh, a middle-eastern form of backgammon, a favorite game in West Jerusalem, too, among Jews who come from Arab countries.

Leave the Old City through the Damascus Gate. The No. 12 bus will take you back to town. If you feel self-indulgent, a taxi will do the same. Don't get into a cab that has no meter, even though the drivers will persuade you to do so. Only metered cabs are allowed on the streets of Jerusalem.

THE SEVENTH WALK

FROM NEW GATE THROUGH THE CHRISTIAN
AND ARMENIAN QUARTERS

*A popular American folk song has spread the misconception
that "There are twelve gates to the city," but in fact there are
eleven, and only seven are open gates. Five of the open gates
were built in the 1500's and are complicated structures with
fine stone ornamentation. By contrast, the New Gate, one of
the two modern gates (the other is Dung Gate), is merely a
breach in the city wall, which appears to have been opened
for the sole purpose of allowing you to enter the Christian
Quarter without having to take one unnecessary step. A brief
walk through this quiet, clean, northwest quadrant of the Old
City leads to the turbulent atmosphere of the Church of the
Holy Sepulchre. The route then turns to the southwest quadrant of the City for an extensive tour of the Armenian Quarter. The Armenians, a people with a painful history, trace
their origin to Haig, a descendant of Japhet, the son of Noah.
Many themes in Armenian history parallel those in Jewish
history: continuous invasions of a land that lay in the path of
conquering armies; repeated destructions and rebirths; forced
exile and a wide-spread Diaspora with strong ties to the
national home. Today, Armenia is one of the United Soviet
Socialist Republics.*

*Take this walk on any day but Sunday and try to start
out before noon so that you can get to the center of the
Armenian Quarter by 2:30 when St. James Cathedral, the
holiest site of the Armenians, opens its doors for prayer
services.*

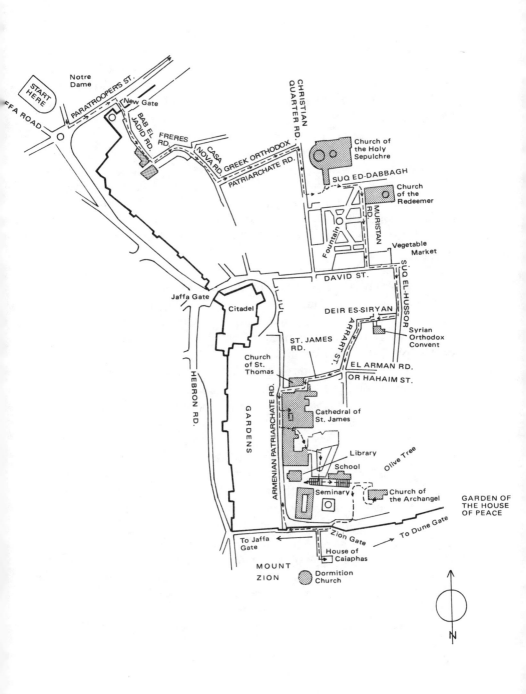

START HERE

Notre Dame

PARATROOPERS ST.

New Gate

FFA ROAD

BAB EL JADID RD.

FRERES RD.

CASA NOVA RD.

GREEK ORTHODOX PATRIARCHATE RD.

CHRISTIAN QUARTER RD.

Church of the Holy Sepulchre

SUQ ED-DABBAGH

Church of the Redeemer

MURISTAN RD.

Fountain

Vegetable Market

DAVID ST.

SUQ EL-HUSSOR

Jaffa Gate

Citadel

DEIR ES-SIRYAN

Syrian Orthodox Convent

ST. JAMES RD.

ARRART ST.

EL ARMAN RD.

OR HAHAIM ST.

Church of St. Thomas

HEBRON RD.

GARDENS

ARMENIAN PATRIARCHATE RD.

Cathedral of St. James

Library

School

Olive Tree

Seminary

Church of the Archangel

GARDEN OF THE HOUSE OF PEACE

To Jaffa Gate

Zion Gate

To Dune Gate

House of Caiaphas

MOUNT ZION

Dormition Church

N

Start this walk at the bottom of **Jaffa Road**, just opposite the northwest corner of the Old City. Turn left into the **Street of the Paratroopers**. About 200 yards from the intersection of these two streets is the **New Gate**, which was cut into the walls of the Old City by Sultan Abdul Hamid in 1889 to give direct access to the Christian Quarter. There are no distinguishing stone features on this gate even though in the late eighteen-hundreds there was still an abundant supply of artisans skilled in stonework. Was the Sultan a boor who had no feeling for the walls of this ancient city? Or, was he strapped for funds? Is it possible that, as a Moslem, he did not choose to call attention to the entrance to the Christian Quarter? We shall never know, for the Sultan made his decisions without benefit of a staff of planning analysts who leave behind them learned essays on the decision-making habits of their boss.

However, you can see the pockmarks of bullets in the stones of the gate. The lovely buildings that you just passed on the Street of the Paratroopers and which you can see from your position in front of New Gate are similarly pockmarked. The plaque on the wall to the right of the gate tells part of the story of the battles that took place on this street during the War of Independence. On July 17, 1948, the underground forces of Lehi entered New Gate, planning to meet the forces of the Haganah who were trying to enter Zion Gate on the south side of the Old City, and Etzel who were supposed to break through Jaffa Gate. This was *Operation Kedem*, or Antiquity, the last Jewish attempt to recapture the Old City, and a total failure. The Arabs had expected an attack and were prepared with a large concentration of forces. Not knowing when the attack would begin they opened a violent bombardment along the whole length of the walls and stopped the advancement of the Jewish forces at every gate. At New Gate they built a roadblock of wood and shavings and ignited it with a shell.

In another battle of that war Arab forces moved down this street in an attempt to conquer West Jerusalem. The Jewish forces turned them back from their outpost in the **Notre Dame Monastery**, that large turreted building on the other side of the street. The monastery was severely damaged and no repairs could be made throughout the period when the City was divided for the building was in West Jerusalem, only 40 yards from the Arab Legionnaires stationed on the walls of the Old City opposite. In the mid-70's the monastery was repaired and converted into a modern hotel for Christian pilgrims.

When you enter the Christian Quarter you will be on **Bab el-Jadid Road**. At the end of this street, turn left into **Freres Road**. This street turns right into **Casa Nova Road**. The **St. Theodori Convent** on your right bears the Greek "taphos" sign which you have already seen on the Greek Orthodox cemetery gate on Mount Zion. You will see it again and again on buildings along this stretch of the walk, particularly when you turn left into the **Greek Orthodox Patriarchate Road**. The road is lined with residences and institutions occupied by members of the Greek Orthodox Church, just as St. Francis Street is occupied by Franciscan Catholics and their institutions, the Street of the Copts by Coptic institutions, and so on. An index of street names in the Christian Quarter is also a comprehensive list of all of the various churches in Christiandom that have established rights in and to Jerusalem. This allocation of space by sect reaches an absurd climax in the Church of the Holy Sepulchre toward which you are slowly making your way.

All along this street can be found excellent examples of some of the details which characterize the architecture of the Old City. Windows and doors must provide access and light but must also keep out thieves and marauders and so the actual openings, while often set in a spacious arch, are small, strongly constructed and easily closed and bolted. The wood used was tough and well seasoned and often reinforced by bands of wrought iron. Windows are invariably safeguarded by strong wrought iron bars or grilles and are a decorative feature of the buildings, but the traditional iron work is heavy and never treated in a frivolous manner as it sometimes is in the newer sections of the city. Small balconies are constructed of wood and enclosed to form oriels and are designed as integral parts of the building, not as afterthoughts. These oriels were constructed in order to ensure that women could view public processions taking place in the street without themselves being exposed to view... There is the taphos again, on that arch over the street just ahead.

At the end of this street, turn right into **Christian Quarter Road**. There are many Armenian shops in this area although Armenians do not live in the Christian Quarter. Notice that the pavement stones are striated. These are the stones of a Byzantine street, which was revealed recently when the Municipality pulled out the relatively modern stone paving to install a new sewage system in the Christian Quarter.

Turn into the first opening to your left, **St. Helena's Road**. After a few steps you will reach the outer courtyard of the **Church of the Holy**

Sepulchre. From ground level you cannot see the church in its entirety; except for this southern facade the building is concealed from view by the many monasteries and chapels which have been built around it by any church group that was given an opportunity to do so. The interior of the church has also been divided among different Christian sects. Each group jealously guards its domain from encroachment by others and will allow no overseeing agency to make decisions regarding repairs, maintenance, and design for the benefit of the church as a whole that might impose constraints on the design or utilization of the specific group's territory. Repairs to the building that are necessary to prevent the collapse of the fabric of the church must therefore be done in bits and pieces and there has never been a time in recent memory when the church has been free of scaffolding, ladders and piles of tools.

Generations of scholars and archaeologists have deduced that the site of this church lay outside the Second Wall of the Second Temple Era and thus was not within the boundaries of the City of Jerusalem during the time of Christ's crucifixion. Therefore, it is entirely possible that he was buried here, for according to Jewish law, no burials could take place within the confines of the Holy City. There is no question that this is the site of an ancient burial ground for many burial caves have been found underneath the church. It is known that in ancient times executions took place close to the burial tombs. This, then, is assumed to be the site of both the Crucifixion and the tomb of the Holy Sepulchre. In the *Gospel According to John* (19:17) it is written, "And He, bearing His cross went forth into a place called the place of a skull, which is called in the Hebrew Golgotha." The hill called Golgotha comes from the Hebrew word for skull, *gulgolet*, which, translated into Latin, is rendered Calvary. Thus tradition holds that Jesus ascended the Via Dolorosa to reach the hill of Calvary, and the last four Stations of the Cross are to be found within the church.

The place name "Skull Hill" derives from an ancient legend that Adam's skull was buried here. The hill itself is no longer distinguishable under the church but pieces of it are exposed in the underground chapels of the church. The Romans in the fourth century thought the place suitable for the construction of a Forum and a Capital. The site was levelled by filling in the spaces among the rock, the promontory and the tombs. Early Christians were forbidden to visit the place but they kept its memory sacred and returned to it when Christianity became the dominant religion during the early Byzantine period.

Originally a group of small separate churches rising on the holy sites of the fourth century and after, the church received its present form in the time of the Crusaders who erected one large Romanesque church to embrace the chapels covering the several sites.

The Romanesque facade of the building is of particular interest. The upper storey forms a double portal, the lintels of both doors being adorned with bas-reliefs of the twelfth century. The grey marble facing on the column to your right should be erased from your memory of this noble entrance.

Just inside the entrance is a slab of red limestone surrounded by tall candlesticks. This is the Stone of Unction where Jesus was annointed after being taken down from the Cross (if you are Greek or Orthodox) or the place where Jesus' body was embalmed (if you are a Roman Catholic).

You will find your way around the Church without too much difficulty if you will bear in mind that the interior is divided into two principal parts, the Rotunda and the Greek Orthodox cathedral. If you start walking into the church from the left you will pass the wall of the cathedral on your right, enter the Rotunda, walk between the small shrine covering the tomb of Jesus, and the entrance to the cathedral, round the other side of the cathedral, and leave the church through the same entrance.

It is a dark, gloomy church and to really enjoy it you have to develop a taste for Middle Eastern hanging lamps decorated with colored glass and for cluttered chapels. Each of them is occupied by another sect; only the Protestants are barred from praying here. The Greeks occupy the major portion of the building because areal assignments were made by the Turks whose interests in Jerusalem were best served by the sect that was a loyal part of the Ottoman Empire.

As you wander through the church and its chapels you will see a number of places where the original Crusader vaults and piers and bare stone facings have been spared the restorer's hand. Only then can you begin to understand how magnificent this church must have been in the twelfth century. We must, however, not be too harsh in our judgment for this church has suffered fire, earthquake and invasion and thus could not avoid a series of hasty and ill-conceived reconstructions. We certainly must not be as harsh as Herman Melville who wrote in the diary he kept on his travels, "The Holy Sepulchre — ruined dome — confused and half-ruinous pile. — Labyrinths and terraces of mouldy

The Rotunda in the Church of the Holy Sepulchre: a once and future view

grottos, tombs and shrines. Smells like a dead-house, dingy light. All is glitter and nothing is gold. A sickening cheat."

Look for the splendid Corinthian capitol from the fourth century which lies in the long passageway just beyond the Rotunda which you must pass in your circuit of this building. Just beyond this passageway there is a staircase leading down into the Armenian chapel. Look for the crosses carved into the stone walls of the chapel by Armenian pilgrims. These are simple stone crosses; the ones you will see on the walls of the Armenian cathedral later on in this walk are as numerous, but far more elegant. The last stop on the circuit is a flight of steep, narrow, and slippery stairs leading down from the Calvary. In order to ascend, turn the corner and go up the stairs to the right of the Stone of Unction. The Calvary is a platform supported mainly by vaulting. Here you can see the hole in which the cross of the crucifixion is said to have been placed.

When you leave the church, turn left into a street called **Suq ed-Dabbagh,** the Street of the Dyers.

You are now in a section of the City known as the **Muristan,** or hospital, after the hospital of St. John, which once stood here and was the original institution of the Knights of Malta. The Muristan is now a Greek Bazaar. Its wares are no different from other bazaars in the Old City; its only distinction is the geometrical pattern of its streets.

Up ahead, on **Muristan Road,** is the **Lutheran Church of the Saviour,** built in 1898 by Kaiser Wilhelm II. You are now going to be asked to ascend the narrow spiral staircase of the church's belltower to see the interrelationship of the several parts of the Old City that you cannot grasp easily from ground level. Since these walks include other opportunities to see the City from on high, do not attempt it if you feel very tired. But since the view is so magnificent and the climb itself an unusual experience, it is highly recommended to make the effort. You, the hardy climber, will catch your breath at the top of the belltower and then look out of the first portico, facing east. Notice the contrast between the newly reconstructed Jewish Quarter, on your right, with its bold effort to recapture the traditional building patterns of the Old City, and the truly traditional roofscape of the Moslem Quarter just ahead, with its old stones and interconnected buildings that possess that variety and richness that a planned community can rarely attain.

Through the next portico you can see the shape of the Church of the Holy Sepulchre as a unity rather than as a series of disconnected parts. The west portico opens onto a view of the Muristan's special road system. The square to your left contains a cluster of stone shapes, which, depending on your tastes, can be considered to be either "very interesting" or gross. This is a fountain erected in honor of Kaiser Wilhelm and placed in the path he followed on his way from Jaffa Gate to lay the cornerstone of the Lutheran church. The Armenian Quarter, which borders the Jewish Quarter, can be see from the south portico.

The walk down the spiral staircase is really not so bad and the fact that it contains 178 steps should instil you with a touch of pride. The Lutheran church itself is a good place to rest; its quiet and good taste provide the serenity lacking in the Church of the Holy Sepulchre.

Amateur archaeologists are expected to look for and find remnants of the Second Wall of the Second Temple in the courtyard of the Lutheran Church, which was uncovered during a dig in 1968.

Across the street of the church is a shop that specializes in sheepskin products: rugs, mini-, midi- and maxi-coats, jackets and slippers. This is a good place to see whether this characteristic Jerusalem product suits your fancy and/or your pocketbook. Be sure to smell before you buy, as some of the sheepskins need a special treatment of cleaning fluid before their odor stops attracting other sheep.

When you leave the sheepskin shop look for a triumphal arch that indicates the end of the bordering streets. It is another ornament built to honor Kaiser Wilhelm. The triumphal arch, known throughout the countries of the Mediterranean as a fitting symbol to mark the arrival of a great ruler, was built for the Kaiser by the Greek Orthodox Church, even though the Kaiser represented the Lutherans. The Greeks and the Germans were allies up to the First World War; the Greek king was a Hohenzollern. There have been many times in Jerusalem's history when political interests proved to be more important than religious differences.

Then walk down the broad, sunny, and scrubbed-looking **Muristan Road.** This street is also known as the **Goldsmiths' Market,** and here you can visit the shops of those Armenian jewellers who still work by hand.

Most of the jewelry shops in the bazaars of the Old City are owned by Armenians. Often, photography equipment is displayed side by side with the jewelry. For generations, the Armenians in the Middle East have held a semi-monopoly in these two trades. Formerly famous for hand-worked gold and silver, today these shops display only mass-produced souvenirs. But these same shop windows are now symbols of the "new look" in religion; Maltese crosses sit next to Jewish stars and both are interspersed with mother-of-pearl replicas of the Dome of the Rock. But on Muristan Road Armenian artisans still practice their ancient craft.

The gold bracelets in all the shop windows are prominently displayed because they perform the same function in the Middle East as a bank does in the West. Families invest their savings in gold bracelets, which the women wear proudly as signs of their menfolk's financial success.

Glimpses into the open courtyards between the shops will reveal, at the right time of the day, tiny tables and stools used by neighborhood men playing sheshbesh out in the open on their off-hours. The Mediterranean courtyard is an extension of the parlor.

At the bottom of the street you will pass an antique shop where you can still buy an ossuary. Ossuaries are stone boxes which were used for storing the bones of the dead in the Second Commonwealth after the corpses had decomposed in their burial caves, such as those you visited on the First Walk.

The last few yards of Muristan Road are covered by a series of vaults that are heavy enough to support a substantial building. Such vaults usually indicate building plans abandoned for any one of a number of reasons. Since the symbol of the German Empire — a lean-looking eagle — is carved on the front of the first vault it can be assumed that Kaiser Wilhelm had an ambitious project in mind which the vaults would eventually support. But there was no time — the Empire lasted less than two decades after his visit to Jerusalem.

Muristan Road ends with a wrought iron gate, and you are now on **David Street.**

This is the midway point of this walk. If you are tired turn right and walk on David Street, the main shopping thoroughfare of the city, till it brings you to Jaffa Gate. If you are not tired turn left and walk through the bazaar. You will soon come to a huge vegetable and fruit market housed in a Crusader building with the vaults and thick supporting columns (piers) typical of Crusader architecture. You will find many varieties of produce that are native to the Middle East and only rarely attainable in the West. Since produce cannot be brought by truck from the farm to the Old City markets, the donkeys standing on what might be thought of as a loading platform serve that purpose.

David Street suddenly becomes **Suq el-Bazaar Road.** Turn into the
first opening on your right, **Suq el-Hussor Road,** or the **Straw Market.**
Wander through the mounds of straw products. The best buys, and the
most unusual, are the woven twig baskets. Suq el-Hussor Road
continues beyond the Straw Market in a set of stairs covered by vaults.
A bit further on your right, the half-arch opening of the Assyrian Convent Road, **Deir es-Siryan Road,** is partially supported by a Saracen
column decorated with a motif used extensively by the Mamelukes
some time between the twelfth and fifteenth centuries.

The Assyrian Convent Road turns into **Ararat Street,** named after
the mountain upon which Noah's ark landed at the end of the flood.
Ararat is traditionally thought to be in the heart of Armenia and the
shape of the mountaintop is the form used for Armenian church domes.
This street brings you into the sunshine once again. Its bordering buildings are blissfully cool in the summer and wickedly cold in the winter.

Turn left and you will see before you the **Syrian Orthodox Convent.** The Syrian Church has influence not only in what is now the
country of Syria but throughout a vast area of the Middle East. It is the
only group that still uses the ancient Aramaic language, not only in
their services but in their daily speech as well. Aramaic was once the
prominent language of the Middle East (it is the language in which the
Talmud was written) but, except for this sect, it hasn't been used as a
spoken language since the ninth century. The Syrian Church insists that
Jesus' last supper took place here, in what is assumed to be **St. Mark's
House,** instead of in the Coenaculum on Mount Zion, as is assumed by
other churches. (You visited the Coenaculum on your Second Walk.) It
was the metropolitan of this church who first purchased the Dead Sea
Scrolls when their value was still unknown.

When you leave the Convent look at the top of the buildings that
border the road and you will see the efforts which have been made to
bring a little green into the stony Quarter.

Turn left and continue walking along the staired street. Notice the
green metal address markers at each door. They were assigned by the
Municipality after the Six-Day War, when the first effort was made
to identify each house for efficient service supply. Previously, each
house had been identified by a series of numbers, all of which still
remain painted in various positions around each doorway. These
numbers have accumulated over the years as each ruling government
attempted to impose some sort of order on the labyrinths of the City.

The staired street turns left again. The stairs are all ascending for you are climbing the eastern slope of Mount Zion. This area is populated entirely by Armenians. Their homes are constructed around a spotlessly clean central courtyard which often contains a small garden thrusting forward among the stones of the pavement. If any of the doors are open, peek into the courtyard; if not, you will get a chance to see this typical Mediterranean form of development in the residential areas of the St. James Convent.

Continue along Ararat Street. At one point, it meets **Al Arman Road**, the Armenian Road, and here you can see where the boundaries of the Armenian Quarter and of the Jewish Quarter merge. Both Quarters claim this street; it is also called **Or Hahaim Street**, Hebrew for the "light of life." In the street sign the conflicting claims end in a draw, with both street names accorded formal acceptance. Mixed population groups have always lived on the peripheries of the various quarters.

Now, turn into **St. James Road**, named in honor of Jesus' disciple, the first bishop of Jerusalem and one of the first Christian martyrs; his home on Mount Zion, according to Armenian tradition, became the center of Christian life in Jerusalem after the Ascension. This street twists about a good deal and at the beginning of its last twist you will see, on your right, massive stones surrounding pointed archways that have been sealed up. These are the remains of the Crusader **Church of St. Thomas**. The Crusaders dressed their building stones with an indented margin all along the border, as did King Herod. It is easy to distinguish between the coarse Crusader stones here and the sophisticated stone work of the indented Herodian blocks. Technology and art do not necessarily progress as time marches on. This church had a long narrow window, on the corner, similar to those found in the walls of the City itself. Was the window used for defense, or was the form merely traditional?

St. James Road eventually ends in the **Armenian Orthodox Patriarchate Road**. Turn left and walk under the arched street. The splendid building spanning the street directly ahead is part of the living quarters of the Armenian Patriarch, whose residence is connected to **St. James Convent**, the large building on your left.

Stand opposite the Convent where you can best see the entrance facade. St. James Convent (Couvent Armenien St. Jacques) is not a single building or even a collection of buildings, but a large and complex compound where Armenians live, worship, socialize, go to school, print books, play soccer, use the library, study for the priesthood, and do their marketing. The Armenians live as a people separate and distinct from their neighbors. Their calendars are printed in the Armenian language, they speak Armenian amongst themselves, although many of them know English, Arabic and Hebrew as well. The compound is a separate entity and a deeply religious city, for the church sponsors and supports all the facets of community life. It is entirely surrounded by a wall, but, unlike the wall of Jerusalem, the compound gates are closed each night at about 10 until 6 a.m. and the families who reside within can neither visit elsewhere or receive visitors. This was perfectly acceptable when the entire huge compound housed only a small number of priests, nuns and seminarians. But in 1948, during the War of Independence, when Armenians fled from their homes in other parts of Jerusalem, they were taken in temporarily by the church and given homes in the compound. Most of them have since immigrated to other countries or have found new homes outside the Quarter, but some still remain, and their children, particularly, chafe at the nightly enclosure.

The facade of the convent contains a number of elements typical of Armenian architecture. First, notice that the windows are placed without much care for symmetry. Each is encased in its own iron cage, and each is quite different from the other. The Mameluke decorative motif that you saw on the pillar at the entrance to this Quarter is repeated on the indentations on both sides of the entrance. You can see that the stones used in the entranceway are completely different from those in the facade; indeed the building is comparatively new while the entranceway is fifteenth century. A glazed tile street plaque written in Hebrew, English and Arabic on one side of the entrance is repeated in Armenian on the other side. All of the tiled street signs in the Old City are made by Armenians.

Opposite the convent is a newly-built Armenian Seminary on the site where King Herod's royal gardens once flourished. Before the Seminary could be built the entire site was dug up. An Israeli law specifies that before any new construction can begin anywhere in the Old City the land must be excavated by the Department of Antiquities to yield its buried historical treasure. Everyone is looking for King Herod. Kathleen Kenyon was here but she didn't find him. Neither did the Israeli archaeologists.

It is now time to enter the compound. Notice that there is a smaller door within the large iron door that bars the entrance. The smaller door serves as an emergency exit when the main door is locked for the night. A guard room just off the entrance houses the Patriarch's guards who walk before him and strike their staffs upon the ground to announce his coming. Their uniforms with the mandatory curved swords are in the ceremonial style established in these parts by the Turks, and are worn on holy days.

Walk through the handsome iron gate to enter the courtyard of **St. James Cathedral.** On the wall of the courtyard opposite the facade of the Cathedral you will see a large number of decorative flagstones. These are *khatchkars* contributed over the centuries by Armenian pilgrims. The decorations repeat the pattern of the cross. No two crosses in Armenian art are ever the same and none is fashioned of two simple perpendicular lines. On the walls of the church entrance itself the poorer pilgrims have engraved their own simple offerings to the church. Only the wealthy can afford the "filigreed stone."

On the wall to the left of the main entrance of the Cathedral you will see a pair of ancient clappers, called *nakus.* Church bells were not allowed in Jerusalem until after 1840. These clappers, beaten to a holy rhythm, still call the faithful to prayer.

A heavy cloth is fastened in a roll above the entrance door. During services the door is kept open and the cloth is unrolled so the people who come late can enter the church quietly. This door covering happens to be decorated with an embroidered seven-branched candelabra, or *menorah.*

The cathedral is built in the style borrowed from the Georgians, the Slavic nation whose republic borders Armenia. Four central pillars support the dome, an unusual one because its "bones" have been left exposed. The arches that support the dome form a six-pointed star. The supporting skeleton of a dome is ordinarily hidden from view above a layer of building material.

The intricately carved wooden altar was made in the seventeenth century. Row upon row of chalices, many of them decorated with precious stones, their liner plates balanced within the cup, decorate the church altar. If it is a feast day, some of the finest chalices are brought out of hiding and returned to the secret treasure house right after the services. The Patriarchate has accumulated a vast collection of treasures over the centuries. It is known that they have been hidden in one of the maze of anterooms in the cathedral building but the exact location is known only to the Patriarch and his most trusted aide. Under the joint sponsorship of the Israel Museum and the Patriarchate, these treasures were put on public display for the first time in 1968, but fears for their safety and the huge cost of displaying them allow only infrequent repetitions of this exhibition. If you have arrived in Jerusalem at a time when the Patriarch is willing to risk it again, a visit to the exhibit is a must.

No electric wires reach the Cathedral. It is lit entirely by dozens of oil lamps and candles.

Two carved wooden thrones face the altar. The larger is the chair of St. James, the smaller the seat of the Patriarch who may move over to the larger chair only on the day of his investiture and once each year thereafter on the saint's feast day.

An opening in the wall on your right leads into a smaller church, once the original St. James Cathedral. Look for the few rows of tiles which are quite different from their blue and white neighbors. Each of these tiles illustrate a Biblical event. The method by which early Armenian craftsmen were able to achieve the deep red color, which requires baking at a very high temperature on the same tile with other colors which require a much lower temperature, is a secret that has been lost since the seventeenth century.

Walk over the stone-paved corridor that leads into the main courtyard of the compound. At the far side of the square, on your right, is the Armenian Press which publishes a wide assortment of materials in the Armenian language. An Armenian script was invented in the fourth century for the sole purpose of writing an Armenian Bible. Prior to that Armenian was only a spoken language and all written documents were composed in the languages developed by their neighbors. Armenian is written from left to right rather than from right to left, as are Hebrew and Arabic, and the Armenians point to this fact as an indication of their Indo-European rather than Middle Eastern lineage.

Walk through the arched entranceway on your left. (A Star of David is carved into the wall at the end of the vaulted passageway.) Turn right into a typical Armenian courtyard. A garden grows in the center and all the individual housing units open onto the garden. This is the residential court of the priests. At the back of the court (between units 30 and 32) there is a small gate leading onto a broad open space. To your right is the **Gulbenkian Library.**

Turn left and walk down the staired road. It passes the community school where boys and girls have always studied together, an extraordinary practice in the Old City. At the bottom of the stairs there is another wall with a small square opening. Lower your head and enter the court of the **Convent of the Olive Tree,** named after the ancient tree enclosed by a stone fence on your right. Armenian tradition holds that this is the tree to which Jesus was tied when brought before Annas, the father-in-law of the High Priest Caiaphas, who was really the power behind the priestly throne.

This courtyard is reserved for nuns. Young Armenian women do not become nuns; only those women who have completed their family responsibilities are allowed to devote themselves to service to the community. The nuns are the caretakers of the **Church of the Archangel** which can be reached by following the small passageway opening into the courtyard. Small churches in the compound are used for family celebrations and simple Sunday masses, while the Cathedral is reserved for major events in the church calendar. In the afternoon hours someone will be available to open the church door for you and show you around.

Leave the nun's courtyard and turn left. The small gate ahead takes you out of the Armenian compound and places you squarely in **Nebi Daoud Square. Zion Gate** is on the far right.

There are references to Bab Sihyun, the Gate of Zion, as far back as the tenth century. It is not known whether this is the site of that more ancient gate, but a gate must have stood nearby even in the days of the Romans. In 1894 the medieval door attached to the Gate was blown down in a storm, revealing a memorial stone to an anonymous soldier of the Roman Empire who had fallen in the year 115 A.D. during an ancient battle for Jerusalem.

The gate leads into the Jewish Quarter as well as the Armenian Quarter. In the Middle Ages, the keys to the gate were entrusted into the hands of the Jews, who were responsible for locking it each night. During the 1948 War of Independence the Gate changed hands three times. Through the Gate's bullet-scarred archway passed the last survivors of the Old City when the Jewish Quarter finally fell.

The simple gatehouse entrance that forms a right angle with the City wall gives no hint of its diverse structural elements — the rampart platforms and porches and the internal L-shaped chamber. Stone stairwells ascend from the lower level to the upper level of the gatehouse and lead to a network of soldiers' barracks. Jordanian soldiers lived in this gatehouse for twenty years, guarding the entrance to the Old City. You can still see their regimental colors fading on the left-hand wall just beyond the entranceway. A tablet on another wall of the gatehouse tells the story of the twenty-two soldiers of the Harel Brigade of the *Palmach* who, immediately after taking part in the conquest of Mount Zion in May of 1948, broke through the Zion Gate to establish contact with the besieged Jewish Quarter. They were battle-weary and had only the most simple weapons. The inscription asks all those who pass through the Gate to remember these men. Leave the Old City through Zion Gate. You are now on **Mount Zion.**

The architects of Sultan Suleiman covered the face of the gate with traditional Ottoman ornamentation, half-capitals supporting stone-twined balls, carved brackets and medallions. Plain square battlements rim the parapet, but the center battlement is topped by a fine Corinthian capital.

Your last stop on this walk is the **House of Caiaphas,** an Armenian monastery. Its entrance is on the left of the road, a few yards past Zion Gate. If the iron entrance is locked, knock. Sooner or later someone will appear to let you in.

Caiaphas was the High Priest at the time of Jesus' condemnation. Then, the wealthy and the mighty of the kingdom lived in the Upper City, of which Mount Zion was a part. It was a common practice for the High Priest to hold conferences with his colleagues in the chambers of his own home. The *Gospel According to Mark* describes one such council: "And they led Jesus to the high priest; and all the chief priests and the elders and the scribes were assembled..." Witnesses were brought in to testify against Jesus, but their testimony was inconsistent. "And the high priest stood up in the midst, and asked Jesus, 'Have you no answer to make? What is it that these men testify against you?' But he was silent and made no answer. Again the high priest asked him, 'Are you the Christ, the Son of the Blessed?' And Jesus said, 'I am; and you will see the Son of man sitting at the right hand of Power, and coming with the clouds of heaven.' And the high priest tore his mantle, and said, 'Why do we still need witnesses? You have heard his blasphemy. What is your decision?' And they all condemned him as deserving death."

The Pilgrim of Bordeaux, an anonymous but literate traveler to Jerusalem in 333 A.D., describes the ruins of the palace of Caiaphas which he found on this site. The monastery you see today was built in the fifteenth century. It suffered so much damage during the past two decades that only a few elements of its former beauty remain. In a small, well-proportioned court are buried the Armenian Patriarchs under heavily embellished arcades. Pay special attention to the Armenian tiles, their famous blue-green glazes chipped and broken by war.

The new church, now being built on the site, is destined to be taller than its prominent neighbor, the **Dormition Church**, and will, therefore, be an important new element in the Jerusalem skyline.

You are now faced with a choice. You may go home by taking either the No. 18 bus outside the Jaffa Gate or the No. 1 bus inside the Dung Gate. If you choose the former, turn left outside the monastery and walk along the footpath that turns right after passing the southwest corner of the Old City Wall and slopes gently down into the Valley of Hinnom. Nearby is the bus stop and a very short ride will bring you back to the world of commerce in the center of town.

If you choose the latter, turn right outside the monastery and walk along the road that skirts the southern wall of the Old City. On the way you will pass the **Garden of the House of Peace,** a landscaped and labelled exhibition of archaeological finds that runs the length of the wall. When you reach Dung Gate you will have to make another choice. You may go home or continue on the Eighth Walk, which begins at the No. 1 bus stop.

THE EIGHTH WALK

FROM DUNG GATE THROUGH THE
JEWISH QUARTER

*During the War of Independence the Arab Legion made its
way through the Jewish Quarter, destroying each building it
won in bitter house-to-house fighting. When the Quarter
surrendered after a six-month siege there were only a few
score exhausted Jewish soldiers left — and only 1000 civilians,
most of them old people who had remained in their homes,
hoping to be allowed to die in the Old City. In the some
twenty years that elapsed between the destruction of the
Jewish Quarter in 1948 and its recapture in 1967, nothing
was done to clear away the rubble, let alone redevelop the
area. It lay dormant, waiting to be reclaimed.*

*It took more than ten years of frenzied building activity
to complete the bulk of the reconstruction work. During that
decade the Jewish Quarter looked very different than it does
today. Heaps of rubble and shattered buildings lay everywhere, and in their midst, here and there, new buildings were
rising on top of the old. Masons could be seen sitting on the
ground and carving stones; donkeys laden with black leather
bags full of rubble were plodding back and forth from ruins
to dumping ground; workmen were laying pipes and pulling
cables. The confusion was more apparent than real; backing it
up were mounds of detailed drawings, maps showing every
stone above ground and below, and the earnest concentration
of scores of people of all ages and persuasions who had come
to the Jewish Quarter to take part in building it anew.*

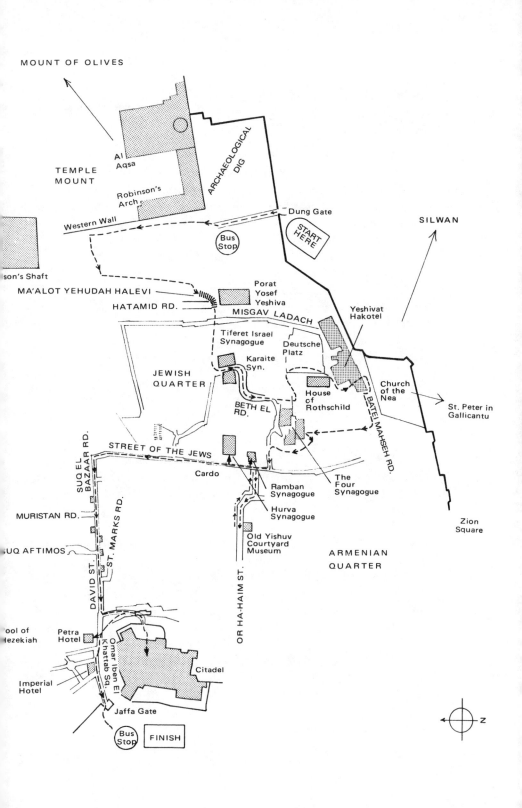

MOUNT OF OLIVES

TEMPLE
MOUNT

Al
Aqsa

Robinson's
Arch

ARCHAEOLOGICAL DIG

Western Wall

Dung Gate

SILWAN

Bus
Stop

START
HERE

...son's Shaft

MA'ALOT YEHUDAH HALEVI

HATAMID RD.

MISGAV LADACH

Porat
Yosef
Yeshiva

Yeshivat
Hakotel

Tiferet Israel
Synagogue

Deutsche
Platz

JEWISH
QUARTER

Karaite
Syn.

Church
of the
Nea

St. Peter in
Gallicantu

BETH EL
RD.

House
of
Rothschild

BATEI MAHSEH RD.

STREET OF THE JEWS

SUQ EL BAZAAR RD.

Cardo

Ramban
Synagogue

The
Four
Synagogue

Zion
Square

MURISTAN RD.

ST. MARKS RD.

Hurva
Synagogue

...UQ AFTIMOS

DAVID ST.

Old Yishuv
Courtyard
Museum

OR HA-HAIM ST.

ARMENIAN

QUARTER

...ool of
...ezekiah

Petra
Hotel

Omar Iben El
Khattab Sq.

Citadel

Imperial
Hotel

Jaffa Gate

Bus
Stop

FINISH

N

*Every wall or part of a wall that could be used was called
back into service and incorporated into new buildings. Every
stone of any historical or archaeological value was lovingly
saved, marked and put on view. Road engineers who
normally love to tear down buildings and pour asphalt over
their remains were not allowed to touch the narrow, twisting
lanes. The result is the charming neighborhood you will be
visiting today in the southeast quadrant of the Old City
where the Jewish Quarter has been since the Middle Ages.
There are still stretches of the Quarter that have not as yet
been reconstructed so you may need to use some of the skills
acquired on previous walks to find your way. It is best to do
this walk on a non-holy day for the galleries and shops in the
Jewish Quarter are closed on Saturdays and shopping in the
covered bazaar through which you must pass when you leave
the Jewish Quarter isn't much fun on Friday or Sunday,
when the Moslem and Christian merchants, respectively, are
resting.*

The No. 1 bus will take you into the Old City on a road that skirts the
Armenian Quarter. Get off the bus at the station near the **Dung Gate,**
which is nothing more than a hole carved into the Walls of the Old City
by the Jordanians, who needed a new access into the southeastern portion of the Old City since the one at Zion Gate was in the hands of the
Israelis.

Cross to the other side of the road to look at the vast Temple
Mount dig, certainly one of the most exciting archaeological excavations in the world. There are catacombs from the days of Judean kings,
remains of houses dating to King Herod, Byzantine bathhouses and
discoveries from every period of Jerusalem's history, the whole worthy
of a guided tour which is conducted frequently by the Society for the
Protection of Nature. (Remember them from the Fifth Walk?) But
even without a guided tour you should be able to identify the huge
Herodian stones on the lower courses of the retaining wall of the
Temple Mount, which were uncovered in the course of this dig. Midway up the wall and slightly south of center are a few rows of broken
stones jutting out from the surface of the wall. (Your eye has picked

Archaeologists begin to dig near Robinson's Arch

out the right stones if above them you can find four windows, one large and barred, three small and framed in a dome-shaped motif.) These stones, now called **Robinson's Arch**, are all that is left of a monumental row of arches that once spanned the Tyropoeon Valley — in which you are now standing — and connected the Temple Mount with the Upper City to the west; the Jewish Quarter, rising behind you as you look into the excavation, was the Upper City in the days of the Second Temple.

Walk straight ahead and through the entrance to the huge open square in front of the **Western Wall**. On your right there is a ramped pedestrian way leading into one of the entrances to the Temple Mount (another must-do guided tour visit). The sign posted at the bottom of the pedestrian ramp warns Orthodox Jews not to enter the Temple Mount. The reason: they may unwittingly tread upon the Holy of Holies, the innermost sanctuary of the Holy Temple which, according to Jewish Law, only the High Priest could enter and which was forbidden to ordinary mortals. Since no one knows the exact location of the sanctuary, the true believer had best take no chances.

The Western Wall Plaza did not exist before the Six-Day War. All of the pre-1967 photos and line drawings of the Western Wall show bearded Jews crowded into a narrow alleyway. When the soldiers of the Israel Defense Forces entered the Old City in 1967 they followed a maze of alleyways to the Western Wall. Reaching the Wall was the singularly moving event of the Six-Day War for all Jews, religious and non-religious, and so it was decided to enlarge the area as a gathering place for the nation. And indeed, multitudes gather here for all national ceremonies. Many a thirteen-year-old boy is taught how to put on his phylacteries (*tefilin*) beside the Wall. When any group wishes to protest anything, this is the place to do it. The Black Panthers call for social justice here; the immigrants from Russia march here with signs reading, "Let my people go." Although prayer services are a round-the-clock activity at the Wall, the atmosphere is hardly restful.

It is customary to tuck a "kvitel" (a note containing a plea or request) between the stones of the Wall. A visitor who left such a note right after the Six-Day War found that his note had risen much closer to heaven when he returned some years later for a second visit. He wasn't aware that in the intervening time the lower courses of the Wall had been uncovered.

Remember that the Western Wall is nothing but a retaining wall, built at the beginning of the Common Era to contain the man-made Temple Mount. But nobody makes retaining walls like that anymore.

At the far end of the Wall and perpendicular to it there is a building with an arched entranceway, the site of yet another dig into the past. Head toward it. On the way you will pass a public toilet with a sign stating that visiting hours are on Sunday, Tuesday and Wednesday from 8:30 to 3 and on Monday and Thursday from 12:30 to 3. This is not as cruel as it sounds, for the sign refers not to visiting hours to the bathrooms, but to the dig, which you should now enter.

Duck through the low passageway just beyond the entrance. You will find yourself in a long, narrow vaulted room. There is a theory that this was a secret passageway used by the Crusaders to get from the palaces of their kings at the Citadel to the Holy Mount. However, the stones have not as yet been dated so no one can be sure whether the theory is correct.

Walk down the passageway to your right. This area was found only after the Six-Day War when different teams of archaeologists began to work in assorted likely looking spots. One team hit pay dirt here. You can see at which level digging began — always at the point between the black stones below and the light colored stones above. Remember that beneath every level upon which you walk lies another as yet uncovered.

A staircase leads you into a large room dominated by **Wilson's Arch,** named after the English archaeologist who discovered it more than one hundred years ago. This arch was the first of a series of arches that bridged the Tyropoeon Valley and provided a walkway for the Jewish priests (*kohanim*) from their homes in the Upper City on Mount Zion to the Temple Mount. To see how deep the valley was that these arches were built to span you must now look into the lighted grating in the floor next to the arch. The grating covers a very deep narrow pit, called **Warren's Shaft,** after Charles Warren, an Englishman who was responsible for the dig. Warren reached the bedrock upon which Herod's retaining wall was built and which accounts for the Wall's remarkable strength and longevity. You can see the bedrock jutting out of the sides of the shaft near its bottom. Mr. Warren must have been an enormously persuasive boss to have convinced his native diggers to descend into the shaft each working day.

Some newer arches to the right of **Wilson's Arch** were attached to the retaining wall by inserting a stone projecting from the back of the arch into a hole carved into the wall. **Wilson's Arch,** however, was planned and built as part of the Wall. Look at the side of the arch and you will see that its back stone is actually an "outgrowth" of the wall.

Upon leaving the dig, re-cross the Plaza along the side farthest from the Western Wall to reach the staircase with the pretty little lights leading up to the Jewish Quarter. At the foot of the stairs, to the right, you will see a slice of the bedrock upon which Jerusalem is built. The bedrock is the foundation for the house rising directly above it.

As you go up the staircase, called **Ma'alot Rabbi Yehudah Ha-Levi,** more and more of the Temple Mount will come into view and soon you will also see the **Mount of Olives** rising behind it, and the village of **Silwan** to the right of the Temple Mount.

The entrance to the **Porat Yosef Academy (Yeshiva),** the large and complicated modern building to your left, can be found where **Hatamid Road** meets the staircase. The arches on this building are large and quite different from those you will find in the old buildings of the Jewish Quarter. The small scale of the openings in the old buildings are appropriate to traditional stone construction. The grandiose arches in the new building are made possible by modern construction techniques where stone is used merely to "wallpaper" a concrete building. The contrast between the two types of arched openings is particularly aching here, for just opposite the entrance to the academy is the courtyard of a Crusader church with "real" openings in its stone walls.

Misgav La'Dach Street is at the top of the staircase. To the right of the staircase there is an entrance to an archaeological garden, which is really the interior of the Crusader church you peeked into just a moment ago. The openings in the walls of the church frame narrow views of the Mount of Olives.

Next to the garden you can see the works of a particularly good local artist who creates bas relief sculptures in metal.

All around you are the new homes of residents of the Jewish Quarter. You must make friends with the people on the street in the hope that one of them will invite you in for coffee so that you can see how the old parts of the buildings have been adapted for modern use. Try for someone with an apartment that opens onto the roof so that you can see the Quarter from different levels.

Walk to the left on Misgav La'Dach Street and turn in at No. 58, where you will find the home and workshop of an artist who specializes in sculpting naked ladies with floppy muscles. Little ladies are swinging out of the library shelves, middle-sized ladies are cavorting in cribs and on the walls and huge ones are sitting about on the roof, seemingly enjoying this chance to take the sun and indulge in some small talk. You can manage to take one of the little ladies home without too much bother or expense. Ask yourself whether the artist is pro-female or anti. There is plenty of evidence for either point of view.

Back to the head of the staircase and then straight ahead. Soon you will find a staircase on your left that leads to the **Tiferet Israel Synagogue.** It was destroyed in 1948 and the arched opening is all that remains of what was once "the glory of Israel." Rabbi Nissan Beck was responsible for its construction back in 1867, but little progress was made until Kaiser Franz Joseph visited Jerusalem on his way to the opening of the Suez Canal in 1869 and left a generous contribution which enabled Rabbi Beck to complete the cupola that rose above the buildings of the Jewish Quarter four years later. The design of the building was based on the model of round synagogues that predominated in the early centuries of the Common Era, and it is hoped that the synagogue, when reconstructed, will retain its original form.

Follow the road in front of the synagogue as it turns to the right. The first doorway on your right is the entrance to the **Karaite Synagogue.** If it is locked ask someone from the Karaite family living in this building to bring along the key. The entrance to their apartment is opposite the arch of the Tiferet Israel Synagogue.

The Karaites once lived around the courtyard of their synagogue in tiny desolate apartments that matched their humble place of worship. Always on the fringes of the traditional Jewish community, the Karaites were never a large group, and by now few are left in Jerusalem. Their synagogue was the oldest in the Old City, even older than the Ramban's, which was built in 1586 and which you will see later in this walk. Their tradition held that the synagogue was built by Anan ben-David, the founder of the Karaite sect, who immigrated to Jerusalem from Persia in 755 A.D. Anan ben-David was forced to break with the established Jewish community because he did not accept the authority of the *Torah she b'al peh*, or the oral tradition within Judaism. He held that the laws of the written Torah alone were binding and that they should be literally interpreted. This led to a set of customs and ceremonies quite unlike those of the rest of the community. For instance, the Karaites used a scissors for circumcision because of a line from Isaiah: "Make your swords into ploughshares"; since swords is plural, one must use a double knife, hence a scissors. The separation of the Karaites from the mainstream of Jewish life continued through the centuries, in all the lands in which they lived. World War II wiped out all trace of the sect in Europe and at the end of the siege of Jerusalem in 1948, when the Jews were allowed to leave the Old City, only two Karaites were among them.

The Karaite Synagogue is on **Ha-memuneh Street**. At the end of this street, turn left into **Beth El Road**. You'll know you are moving in the right direction when you spot the post office on your right. The road turns to the right and terminates in a small square. On your left there are three stairs which lead into a narrow alleyway covered with a low vaulted ceiling.

Once again in the sun, you must turn to the left. On the wall to your left there is an iron insignia of the Israel Defense Forces and Hebrew lettering set within a stone arch which tells of the soldiers who died during the battle for Jerusalem in 1948. Their bodies were kept in this small courtyard until the Jewish Quarter was recaptured in the Six-Day War, after which their bodies were removed to the common grave on the Mount of Olives, which you saw on your First Walk in Jerusalem.

Up ahead is the **Deutsche Platz**, or German Plaza, which was named after a group of Dutch and German Jews who purchased this land in the latter part of the nineteenth century. At the time, there was much talk among the more enlightened residents of the Jewish Quarter of leaving the Old City and building modern homes outside the wall. These German Jews wanted to prove that the Old City itself could be modernized. They built seventy apartments and rented them out on condition that each family would leave after three years so that as many families as possible would get a chance to live decently, if only for a short period of time. Perhaps it was this taste of better homes that actually spurred the movement of Jews to develop new areas outside the walls. Built by the Austrian branch of the family, the new apartment building was named the **House of Rothschild.** It is the long, low handsome structure, newly rehabilitated, with the Rothschild coat of arms, that marks the western side of the square. Notice that all its windows face the Temple Mount and the cemetery on the Mount of Olives. Most of the residents of the Jewish Quarter had this view constantly before them; modern technology has enabled us to close the view, unfortunately. No one lives in this building today; it has been recycled into an office building for the company responsible for rehabilitating the Jewish Quarter.

If you still have not managed to get an invitation to see the Jewish Quarter from someone's private roof, walk to the building that borders the plaza on its east side, and climb the staircase to see the view from a public observation point.

On the southern edge of the plaza is **Yeshivat Hakotel.** Notice the large iron "screws" that hold this building in place.

Walk through the arched entranceway on the right side of the Yeshiva and you will find yourself on **Batei Mahse Road,** a street lined with a continuous row of "sheltering houses." You are standing on a level slightly higher than the City Wall and looking down at the southern section of Jerusalem. The **City of David** lies before you and opposite it is the **Village of Silwan.** A landmark you have not seen before on these walks lies below you to the right. It is the blue-domed **Church of St. Peter in Gallicantu,** a most lovely place indeed, where people from Holland come to spend a few months in Jerusalem, taking just such walks as you are taking today.

The area between this road and the wall of the Old City has served different functions over the centuries. In Byzantine times it was the site of the **Church of the Nea,** then the largest church in Christiandom. It was destroyed by an earthquake in 746 A.D. Then the site served as a dumping ground and the church was buried under yards and yards of rubble, seemingly forever. When plans were made for the construction of an amphitheatre and park on this site, the archaeologists' bulldozers were called in before the contractors', and the long-lost church was discovered. Amid much consternation, the plans of the amphitheatre were changed in such a way as to enable the visitor to listen to a Mozart trio and peek into the church at the same time.

You are now standing on the edge of the Jewish Quarter. If you look a mere 100 yards to the west you will see a minaret, an Armenian apartment building, a new Jewish apartment building next door and crosses atop three separate towers. Despite the division of the City into four separate and distinct quarters, the populations get mixed up, particularly on the borders between quarters. (If you are tired, leave the Old City through Zion Gate and follow the instructions at the end of the seventh walk to find a bus.)

To continue — walk toward the west and turn right at the first opportunity. You are in **Tiferet Yerushalayim Square.** Straight ahead is a curious group of four underground interconnected rooms, each a separate Sephardic synagogue where once congregants freely moved from one to the other, and on holidays and festivals, each congregation sang at its own pace. To enter the group of synagogues you must descend a temporary wooden staircase and walk into the opening on your left. The first synagogue is named after **Rabban Yochanan ben Zakkai**, who, it is said, prayed here when he realized that the Second Commonwealth was doomed. He asked the Romans for permission to leave Jerusalem with his followers to establish a new center of learning in Yavneh.

The opening directly ahead leads into the oldest synagogue of the four, a small, subterranean apartment called the **Synagogue of Elijah.** The legend has it that some centuries ago, during one of the periods of persecution, the handful of Jews who lived in Jerusalem were in great fear and danger, and could only meet in secret for their community prayers. It happened one Sabbath day that the services could not be held because there were only nine Jews present and a tenth could not be found in order to form a *minyan*, or congregation of ten. Suddenly a stranger appeared, an old man who had never been seen before by any of those assembled. With joy, the worshippers began their prayers. When the service was over and the congregants turned to thank the stranger and invite him for lunch, he had disappeared without a trace. It was clear to the congregants that the stranger was none other than the prophet Elijah. The legend of the Tenth Man, a single human being upon whom the well-being of an entire community depends, reappears in different forms and in different places throughout Jewish history. The niche on the left wall of the room once held Elijah's chair, a richly carved throne which the Sephardic Jews carried with them when they made their way from Spain to Jerusalem in 1492, so that the prophet would not miss his accustomed seat when he came to pray with them in the new synagogue.

Go back to the Ben Zakkai Synagogue. The first arched opening in the wall on your left leads into a small room open to the sky which was used for the community *succa*, the booth required for the Succot Festival. The second arched opening leads to the **Middle Synagogue**, with its columned gallery, where the ladies of the congregation might enter modestly from the street.

Through an opening on the left you can enter the last of the four, the **Istambuly Synagogue**, built on the church pattern you have seen a number of times in Jerusalem: four columns supporting an arch and a dome. The Jews of the Old City didn't have the services of a local architect to design their public buildings. Whenever an architect was imported from Europe by one of the churches nearby he was invited by the Jewish community to assist them with reconstruction and new building.

Next to the golden *bima* of this synagogue you will find a double arched exit. On the other side of the exit there is an inscription taken from the prayer service — the only one not defaced by the Arabs after the War of Independence. It begins: "This is the gateway to God."

Retrace your steps to the top of the wooden staircase leading to the synagogue and jump over the adjoining ledge. Walk in the direction of the huge white stone arch that is seemingly suspended in mid-air. Turn left when you come to a building with a sign reading: "Tzemach Tzedek Chabad." Enter the narrow road beyond the building: **Or Hahaim Street**. People living on this street have tried to introduce greenery to relieve the sometimes oppressive concentration of heavy stone. Peek in at No. 8 (nice address plates on this street) to see the greening of a stone courtyard.

At No. 6 you will find the **Old Yishuv Courtyard Museum** which attempts to portray life as it was lived in the Jewish Quarter prior to 1948 through a display of tools, artifacts, furnished rooms, clothing and photographs. The building that houses the museum is nothing more than a series of rooms that have been used as Jewish dwellings since the 1600's. The courtyard of this house, now covered with a wooden pergola, contains the water cistern and the sewage system. But the courtyard also served a social function as the only common space of all the residents of the building. The housewife hung out her wash and chatted with her neighbors; since there was no neighborhood park the courtyard was the playground for all the children; during times of unrest it served as a hiding-place.

The Old Yishuv refers to the Jewish population in Israel before the First Aliya (wave of immigration) in 1882. Composed mainly of Jews that had been expelled from Spain, the Old Yishuv felt strongly tied to the Ottoman Empire. It was these Jews who, by their continuous presence in the Holy Land, symbolized the link between the Diaspora and Israel. In 1882 there were 24,000 Jews living in Jerusalem. There were Ashkenazim, too, in the Old Yishuv that had begun arriving in 1700 but they were divided among themselves into separate groups, possibly for economic reasons: each group was supported by the Jews remaining in the European country or city of their origin.

It was the Sephardic Chief Rabbi who represented the Old Yishuv before the governors of the Turkish Empire. He was known as the *Rishon le Zion*, "the highest ranking dignitary in Zion." Israel now has two "highest ranking dignitaries in Zion," a chief rabbi for the Sephardim and one for the Ashkenazim. But in pre-Mandate days the Sephardic chief rabbi was the single major dignitary. He dealt with all internal community problems and, as the official representative of the Jews to the governors of Palestine, took his place with the ranking dignitaries of other churches and national groups on all state occasions. The Sephardim always · managed better than did their brethren from Germany and Eastern Europe to get on with their Mohammedan neighbors; they spoke the same language and had, in the Diaspora, lived among Arabs. It is interesting that the Turks did not refer to the Ashkenazim as Jews; they were either Frenchmen, Russians or Germans, depending on their country of origin.

The exhibit shows the three principal rooms in a typical dwelling unit: the kitchen with its separate section for baking and cooking, the living room for "company" and the bedroom for all members of the family. (Count the beds shown in one room and note their different sizes.) Another section of the museum portrays the means of livelihood open to the residents, some of them no longer prevalent, like fortune-telling. The artifacts displayed tell us what life was like for the Jewish inhabitants of the Old City; some of them were even in use at the time the Jews were expelled in 1948.

Retrace your steps out the museum and back to that large white stone arch. You are now on the **Jewish Quarter Road** (The Street of the Jews). Turn right and stop at No. 95/90 where there is a Hebrew sign pointing to the **Ramban Synagogue.** The Ramban, known in the West as Nachmanides, was a great teacher and commentator on the Bible, famed throughout the Diaspora as the wisest of Jews. In his home in Spain the Ramban led an honored and creative life, surrounded by family and students. A common practice of the church in the Middle Ages was to invite a learned Jew to participate with scholarly church-men in a verbal contest on the relative merits of their two religions. The Ramban was invited to such a debate when he was already an old man, won the argument, to his misfortune, and was expelled from his homeland. Together with some devoted disciples he traveled for three years to reach Palestine, then in the hands of the Mamelukes. It was 1267 and there were only two lonely Jewish families in all of Jerusalem. In a letter to his son in Spain, the Ramban wrote: "Only two Jews, brothers, dyers by trade, did I find. And behold, we pressed them and we found a ruined house with marble pillars and a beautiful dome, and we took it (to serve) as a synagogue...and they already began to build, and we sent to the town of Shechem, to bring thence the scrolls of the Law, which had been in Jerusalem and had been smuggled out when the Tartars came, and, behold, they built a synagogue and they will pray there." Thus, a Jewish Quarter was established on the eastern slope of Mount Zion. Before that, during lenient periods of the Moslem hegemony, such Jews as were allowed to live in Jerusalem made their homes in the area now known as the Moslem Quarter in order to be as close as possible to the Temple Mount. Moslem and Jew fought together against the invading Crusaders and suffered defeat together at the end of the eleventh century. The Crusaders destroyed the entire Jewish populace and set fire to their Quarter. Since then, Jews have never returned to that section of the City.

The well-preserved marble pillars of the building indicate that this might have been a Crusader church before the Ramban converted it into a synagogue. Crusader maps of Jerusalem show the Church of St. Martin on this site. When Jews returned to the Quarter in 1967, they searched painstakingly for the Ramban Synagogue; exactly seven hundred years had elapsed since it had been founded. Since every building was buried under rubble and could not be distinguished from its neighbor, old men with vivid memories of the Quarter were brought in immediately to try to pinpoint the spot where digging should begin. It was these pillars, uncovered one by one, that showed the diggers they had selected the right place.

When you leave the synagogue note the minaret built on the same lot in a long-ago Moslem effort to change the character of the Jewish Quarter.

At No. 87 there is a sign: **Etz Hayim Talmud Torah and Yeshiva.** Walk through its entranceway into the courtyard of the **Hurva Synagogue**, now only four broken walls and a few small heaps of rubble. Before 1948 the dome of the Hurva, the most splendid of the 58 synagogues then in the Jewish Quarter, identified the Quarter on the cityscape, just as the domes of St. James identify the Armenian Quarter and the domes of the Holy Sepulchre the Christian Quarter. Grown men who were little boys then recall tearing around the narrow, columned ring that bordered the huge dome, defying gravity while their elders were immersed in prayer inside the synagogue. The Hurva was the community center of the European Jews of Jerusalem, both inside the walls and outside. Here they met their friends, made community decisions, held public assemblies.

In 1699 Rabbi Yehudah Hasid, a disciple of Sabbatai Zvi, the "false Messiah" who claimed that it was time for the Jews to return to Zion, came to Jerusalem from Europe with 400 followers and bought this piece of ground to establish a synagogue and yeshiva. At the time there were only 1,200 Jews living in Jerusalem, all of them Sephardim who had been expelled from Spain in 1492. The arrival of this new group increased the population by 33 percent and by all reports the overcrowding was unbearable. The Ashkenazim couldn't afford to build anything more than a small hut for study and prayer. Their leader died three days later and his followers, unable to take the difficult conditions of life in Jerusalem, dispersed, many of them to Safed where a community of Ashkenazim had existed for hundreds of years. The Moslems who had sold them the property and had never been fully paid were furious and for a hundred years no Ashkenazi dared show his face in the City. In 1820 Jews from Safed began to return to Jerusalem and with the help of Sir Moses Montefiore bought the land outright and built their splendid synagogue.

The Hurva has not as yet been rebuilt simply because no one is quite sure how it should be done. There are two opposing points of view. One holds that the Jewish Quarter should be rebuilt to look as it did twenty years ago; the other claims that the beauty of the Old City lies in the accretion of different architectural forms, one century's style built upon the former century's, and that the forms of the twentieth century should now be added. Until this issue is resolved the Hurva will remain four shattered walls, a broken stone *bima* (lectern) in the center, with patches of Italian marble flooring and an archway on the western wall where once the *aron hakodesh* (ark of the Law) stood.

Across the street from the Hurva Synagogue is a spectacular archaeological find. A few years ago it was decided to hold a competition for the redesign of the main thoroughfare of the Jewish Quarter and its adjacent buildings. The prize-winning design was detailed on hundreds of specification drawings and a contract was duly signed with a contractor. The building workers had been digging for some time when their shovels scraped the dirt off huge paving stones and several broken columns that were lining the pavement. Construction was halted, the archaeologists were consulted and, after learned consultation, they announced that the **Cardo** had been discovered. The news spread rapidly and throngs of knowledgeable Jerusalemites flocked to see the main north-south axis of the Roman garrison town of Aelia Capitolina.

When a discovery of archaeological importance is made during the course of digging the foundations of a new house in the Old City there are two possible courses of action: either the find is photographed and several learned articles are published about it and thereafter it is covered over by the new building; or, the building is redesigned to incorporate the find, and keep it open to view. There was never any question that the Cardo must be kept open to the public and so all of the expensive plans were thrown out and the design process began anew. The building now has an open arcade on the ground floor and the Cardo can be seen at its far end.

Keep walking up Jewish Quarter Road and soon you will find a structure spanning the street. When you pass it, turn around to see the building's arched windows framed by carved domes. This was once the **Hospice of Rabbi Baruch.** Its height was advantageous to the Jewish unit garrisoned here in 1948 in order to control the access street into the Jewish Quarter. Nonetheless, it could not be held.

As you walk further up the street you will notice that its character changes. We associate its smells and sights with Middle Eastern poverty. The Jews, who resided here before the Arabs who now occupy the street, lived under the same difficult conditions in overcrowded and unheated buildings which were so old that even minimal service standards could not be maintained. It was because of these extremely difficult living conditions that many Jews at the turn of the century began to leave the Old City for points west, just as Arabs began to leave the walled City for points north and west.

At the end of Jewish Quarter Road turn left into **Suq el-Bazaar Road**, the covered market, where only a small amount of light can enter the street and its bordering stalls. These shops were built as warehouses, the merchants displaying only a sample of their wares outside and changing the display to suit the whims of the passing customers. All of the small lanes leading away from this street and deeper into the market were once separate markets that specialized in a single category of produce, such as spices or textiles. Now all the market streets have shops catering to a multitude of needs and only the street names, i.e. Spice Market Street, retain the flavor of the older distribution system. On the wall opposite is a particularly handsome street sign in Arabic and English. Notice that the Hebrew section has been ripped off.

An excellent shop for antiquities and assorted odds and ends that need only a brisk polishing to make them look magnificent is the **Oriental Museum**. Mr. Abou Eid is particularly interested in ancient coins, most of which he buys from peasants in the Hebron Hills who come upon them as they till the soil. He keeps a large assortment of books of the coins of the country for handy reference in the buying and selling process.

Prices are high at **Rashid Sinokrot and Sons**, on your left but the inlaid mother-of-pearl pieces, imported from Damascus, are fine to look at and even more expensive elsewhere.

The street you are walking on now is called **David Street**. It is the major shopping center of the Old City. David Street is built on a valley that bordered the north wall of Jerusalem during the days of the Hasmoneans. The wall began at the Citadel and terminated at the Temple Mount. Just as did later wall builders, the Hasmoneans looked for an appropriately deep and well-situated valley and then built their wall near the top of the rise bordering the valley. The valley supplements the defensive power of the wall, just as the Valleys of Hinnom and Kidron add to the strength of the present city walls. When you come to **St. Mark's Road** on the left, you will see stairs climbing steeply up the mountainside that supported the north wall of the city when Judah Maccabee's descendants ruled Jerusalem.

There are a number of shops that are wonderful for browsing on this stretch of David Street. Just opposite an opening on your right — **Suq Aftimas** — is a nameless shop well known for its hand-embroidered Arab dresses. The peasant women who make them receive only a small fraction of the price you will be charged. After only a casual inspection of the goods you will be able to distinguish between machine-embroidered new dresses and richly hand-embroidered used dresses. Even if you have never worn a used dress, the fashion potential of any one of them is practically unlimited. Nearby at **Khaled Baraket's** you can buy just the embroidered parts of the old dresses, if you cannot overcome your prejudices against used clothes.

As you walk down this street you may get a chance to see men and women trying to sell their family jewelry to "sidewalk" merchants.

David Street terminates in a square named after **Omar ibn el-Khattab**, the caliph who conquered Jerusalem in 637 and, among other important things, gave the Armenians religious jurisdiction over the Christian sects then residing in the city. In an edict to the inhabitants of Jerusalem he stated, "Let not their (the Christians') religion be subjected to scorn, and let no harm befall upon any of them. Let none of the Jews live with them in Jerusalem, but only those who through Abu Huneir undertook submission to the law of Islam, as did the Armenian people... Alongside this nation, the Copts, the Assyrians and the Abyssianians too in Jerusalem fall under the religious jurisdiction of the Armenian Patriarch...Thereupon, the Prince of the Faithful summoned the congregation of Mar Jacoub (St. James) and the inhabitants of Jerusalem, so that they pay their taxes as all citizens pay."

You are now reaching the end of your walking tour through Jerusalem, and are ready for a final overview of the City which you have come to know almost intimately. Ironically, this can be done only by climbing the staircase to the topmost level of the roof of the seedy **Petra Hotel** on your right. It will take your breath away, literally and figuratively. Walk to the only accessible railing and look down into the **Pool of Hezekiah**. An unsightly rent in the fabric of the city, it is used as a garbage dumping ground by the residents of the buildings bordering it. But in ancient times, when it was even larger than it is today, the

A view to the southeast from a rooftop near the Pool of Hezekiah. The large quadrangle on the top right is the Hurva Synagogue that was destroyed in 1948. It appears that there has always been a "living stream" flowing down David Street.

pool captured and held the precious rainwater of the winter season for use during the dry summer months. Even though it can perform no similar function today, no one is willing to part with the pool because in The Second Commonwealth period it was part of a system of interconnected waterworks that supported a large urban population. Then it was known as the **Hamygdalon Pool,** "mygdal" being the Hebrew word for tower; indeed the **Phasael Tower,** rising at the edge of the Citadel, can be seen just off to your right.

During the period of the Second Temple, Jerusalem developed toward the north and new northern walls were built to contain the City at different times. Scholars expend a great deal of time and energy trying to find evidence for their own version of where exactly the north wall of Jerusalem lay during the period of Christ. At stake is a major question in the history of the Church: Was Jesus really buried where the Church of the Holy Sepulchre now stands? From your observation point above the Old City you can begin to grasp the bare elements of the problem. As noted in your seventh walk, since no burials are or ever were allowed within the Holy City, the Holy Sepulchre must lie outside of what was then the walled boundary of the City. It is known that the Pool of Hezekiah lay just outside the western wall of the city.

If Jesus were buried at the site of the Church of the Holy Sepulchre, then the western wall of the city would have followed the far line of the pool immediately in front of you, then turned east a few hundred yards beyond the northern boundary of the pool and would have turned north to skirt around the domes of the **Church of the Holy Sepulchre** that now lies within the city on your left.

A number of points regarding this description of the circuit of what is called "The Second Wall of the Second Temple Era" are still open to question, but by now it has been definitely established that the site of the church lay outside the wall. The location of the pool is also known with certainty. Josephus, writing in *The Wars of the Jews* shortly after the events therein described, stated that the Tenth Legion of the Roman Army was camped at the edge of the pool, at just about the spot where you are now standing. During the siege of the city in 70 A.D. the Legion was assigned to the destruction of every trace of this Second Wall, a task which it accomplished well.

Back to today. The characteristic domes of the Old City top the buildings that line the pool. Many of them are heavily tarred to seam the apartments below from the winter rains. Notice the stones that form large arches within the lower levels of the walls of a number of buildings that border the pool. Such arches often indicate that a modern building has been built on top of the remains of an older building. However, these arches are supports built into the lower level of any building which rises above one story in height.

The northern border of the pool is occupied by the **Great Coptic Khan.** Khan is an Arabic word for inn. Each sect with headquarters in Jerusalem built one or several khans to house its own pilgrims. Today this important function is handled by commercial hotels. Where once the presence of co-religionists or co-nationals could make the foreigner feel welcome and at home, today's pilgrim must rely on the physical similarity among hotel accommodations all over the world to provide that feeling of security.

Looking out over the cityscape, you once again face the by-now familiar landmarks that characterize Jerusalem. Beyond the walled city, on the ridge formed by **Mount Scopus — Mount of Olives,** you can see, starting from the left, the **Hebrew University campus,** the **Augusta Victoria Hospital,** the **Tower of the Russian Church in E-Tur** and the **Intercontinental Hotel.** The **Mountains of Moab** are blue in the distance, but a mound of rounded hills at their base seem to repeat the shape and earthen color of the domes of the city stretching toward it. The golden **Dome of the Rock** lies just ahead of you, the twin domes of the **Church of the Holy Sepulchre** are off to your left, and the modern **Lutheran Church of the Redeemer** belltower rises high just in front of it. Had you been standing here prior to 1948 you would also have seen the dome of the **Hurva Synagogue,** now a bulk of shattered stones with a large arch, and your picture of the religious elements of Jerusalem would have been complete.

Off to your right there is a view over the top of Mount Zion, a ridge that continues along the entire western side of the City until it ends approximately where the familiar cone tower of the **Dormition Church** rises up to block your view. Since this is one continuous mountain it is strange that Sultan Suleiman left the southern portion of Mount Zion outside the walls.

Much of the Mount Zion ridge is occupied by Armenians. During the days of the Second Temple this area was the most elegant section of the city, where kings and princes built palaces and royal gardens. Then it was known as the Upper City, as it commanded a higher natural position in the topography of the city than did the Lower City, where the common folk lived. After the Romans conquered Jerusalem the camp of the Tenth Legion occupied most of the Mount Zion ridge, from which they could keep the whole city in view. When paganism was abandoned and Christianity took its place the site of the St. James Cathedral was one of the first established holy places. It was given into the care of the Armenians who were the first national group to embrace Christianity. More and more Armenians settled in the immediate vicinity and by the Crusader period the Armenian Quarter occupied all of the Upper City. Two silvered peaks can be clearly distinguished in the middle of the Armenian Quarter. Their unusual shape is characteristic of all Armenian churches. The larger of the peaks is the dome of **St. James Cathedral**; its pyramid-topped belltower lies further to the left.

Retrace your steps back to the square in front of the hotel, cross the road, and follow the square as it turns to the right. Soon you will find the entrance to the **Citadel**, popularly known as the **Tower of David**, even though King David's Jerusalem was entirely limited to Mount Ophel on the southeastern edge of the Old City. You won't have time on this walk for a tour of the Citadel itself, the strategic element in the City's defensive system for all the rulers of Jerusalem from the Hasmoneans to the Arab Legionnaires. But you should go inside now to see a well-done half-hour slide show with sound track in English that is presented every half-hour. You surely deserve a rest.

Return to the square. A sign reading "Joseph's Patisserie" marks the alleyway between the two wings of the **Imperial Hotel,** which was the grandest hotel in Jerusalem in the late 1800's. Walk into the alleyway and soon you will come upon a stone pillar supporting a light standard. Scan the carvings on the pillar; on the fourth line from the top you can make out the letters LEGX — the Tenth Legion of the Roman Army, that was stationed here just before and for long after the destruction of the Second Temple. Fortunately, the soldiers were fond of leaving traces of themselves wherever they went. Unfortunately, they were all too fond of destroying the places they had conquered.

Leave the alleyway and turn right. Behind an iron fence there is a small graveyard containing two tombs, said to be the resting place of the architects of the city walls and its gates. It seems that Sultan Suleiman was so displeased with his architects for failing to include Mount Zion within the circuit of the walls that he ordered their execution.

Next to the cemetery there is a row of newly renovated shops which are all part of the gatehouse of **Jaffa Gate.** You may leave the City via the gate or via the road next to it on the left. If you choose the road, remember that you are walking on what was, before 1898, a protective moat that once circled the entire **Citadel.** The moat was filled in to make a plaza suitable for Kaiser Wilhelm's ceremonial entrance into the Old City on horseback. (He stayed at the Imperial, of course.) When General Allenby conquered Jerusalem in 1917 it was suggested to him that he make a similar grand entrance. He did enter the City through the road, rather than through the gate, but he dismounted first in an effort to make his entrance into the Holy City as humble as possible.

If you choose to leave the City through the gate, an L-shaped passageway will lead you through the tower to another opening which enters directly onto **Jaffa Road,** one of the principal thoroughfares of modern Jerusalem; the road terminates at this gate, meeting the road from Hebron. In Arabic this gate is called *Bab el Khalil,* the Gate of the Beloved, the Moslem appelation for Abraham, who is buried in Hebron. Above the entrance to the gatehouse there is an inscription: "There is no God but Allah, and Abraham is beloved of Him." Try to find the beautifully carved capital of Crusader origin that is tucked unobtrusively into a wall high up on your left.

Buses and taxis are readily available for the trip home.

Naturally, these walks have not covered all the varied and interesting places which together make up the magic of Jerusalem. You will find suggestions of things you must see, and things you might see in the remaining pages.

DON'T LEAVE WITHOUT SEEING...

The places listed below are not included in any of the walking tours because they should be seen individually, when you have plenty of time and nothing else on the itinerary. If you have come to Jerusalem as part of an organized program, you will probably get to see most of them with your group. If not, be sure to see them by yourself.

The **Knesset** is the Israeli Legislature. It is best to see the building and its works of art with a guide. Organized tours are available on Sunday and Thursday and start every half-hour from 2:30. Have your passport with you or you won't be let in. The security check is quite rigid. Don't be alarmed when you are asked to leave your purse at the entrance. You may take your wallet and passport with you when you enter.

Many of Israel's finest artists were commissioned to produce the paintings and sculptures on the walls of the Knesset. The most spectacular treasure of all are the Chagall-designed Gobelin Tapestries hanging in the Great Hall.

Come again when the Knesset is in session: Monday, Tuesday, 4-8; Wednesday, 11-3, except for the recess from April 16 to May 16 and the two-month break beginning in mid-August. Keep your eye on the Cabinet table which is on the right of the Speaker's dais to try to catch a glimpse of your favorite minister. You may have picked a day when it is his turn to answer questions from the floor.

When you leave the Knesset cross the road in front of the Palombo Gates and have a close look at the huge bronze candelabra which once adorned the more modest first Knesset building. Each branch of the candelabra is covered with relief sculptures depicting different periods in Jewish history.

The only busline to the Knesset is the No. 9. If you get back onto the No. 9 bus heading away from the city you can go right on to the **Hebrew University**, which is only two stops away from the Knesset. The tall buildings you see from the bus are Government offices. The bus goes past these and stops right in front of the University. Your bag or briefcase will have to pass inspection by the keeper of the gate in the fence which was put up only after a bomb placed in the cafeteria by terrorists exploded. Inside the gate, turn left to see the Student's Center and the Planetarium; right to the Administration Building. Walk along the row of buildings extending in a right angle from the Administration Building and look out over the campus lawns to see how students here spend their between-class time. If there is a large crowd, find out what it's all about. Anyone can set up a table outdoors to get signatures for petitions. This often leads to "direct confrontation" between the opponents on an issue.

Enter any of the buildings to see what a classroom here is like. A particularly nice one is the Kaplan Building at the end of the row, where courtyard gardens seem to enter the building. The National Library blocks the row. Go to its basement floor for some lunch at the cafeteria and sample what the students eat. There is usually an exhibit of rare books on the second floor.

If you have the strength, continue on the path from the National Library to see the other buildings on the campus. The views from either side of the road are splendid. If you persevere you will get to the Geography-Geology Building, which has a fine, small display of the natural rocks of Israel, and to the famous, white, squat-domed synagogue which is so much a part of the Jerusalem landscape. You are now at the farthest end of the campus, and in front of you, as you leave the synagogue, are the students' dormitories.

For security purposes, buses that service the city itself may not enter the campus. To get back to town you will have to get the campus bus that stops near the synagogue, take it to the Administration Building and transfer to the No. 9 or 16 bus.

On your way back to town, stop at the **Israel Museum**, only one bus stop away from the University. It is not open to the public on Tuesday until 4. As you leave the bus, walk to the **Shrine of the Book** on your right. After a thorough visit here, climb the long, broad staircase to the Museum's main building. The archaeological exhibits are particularly worthwhile, although the permanent collection of paintings is not on as high a level as that of the Metropolitan in New York or the Art Institute of Chicago. Nevertheless, the collections of artifacts and ceremonial objects are beautifully displayed and the building itself is one of the most handsome in Israel. More interesting than any of the permanent collections, however, are the special exhibits which the Museum sets up for limited periods. There is always at least one special exhibit, invariably beautifully arranged.

The Museum has a cafeteria serving excellent food, but the prices are high.

A specially good time for an extra visit to the Museum is Tuesday night, when the magnificent **Billy Rose Sculpture Gardens** are illuminated and when an old art film is shown in the Museum auditorium.

If archaeology is your thing you must also visit the **Rockefeller Museum** across the street of the northeast corner of the Old City.

Two adjacent mountains among the hills of Jerusalem near the outskirts of the City have been set aside as a place of mourning for the nation's dead. The first, **Har Herzl**, is the national cemetery, where those whom the nation chooses to honor are buried. The second, **Har Hazikaron** (The Hill of Remembrance), is the site of the memorial to those who died in Europe during the Second World War in Hitler's final solution to the Jewish problem. Set aside a few hours to visit both of them.

Any bus route along **Herzl Boulevard** will let you off in front of the entrance to the Har Herzl Cemetery. Inside is the simple, black marble tombstone of Theodore Herzl, the founder of modern Zionism. A small museum near the entrance contains his papers and is worth a visit.

Walk along the paths to find the burial place of Ze'ev Jabotinsky. Close by you will see the graves of Israel's former Prime Ministers Levi Eshkol and Golda Meir. The paths and open spaces around the graves are finely landscaped and you will be surprised to see that the cemetery serves as a park for the surrounding communities. On any clear Saturday afternoon the place is full of neighborhood children.

The national military cemetery lies along one of these paths. Any passerby will direct you. You will see the graves of those who fell in defense of the country both between and during the War of Independence (1948), the Suez Campaign (1956), the Six-Day War (1967), and the Yom Kippur War (1973). Read the markers on the graves. Each cites the soldier's country of origin, and there are almost as many countries represented as there are nations on the map.

As you leave Har Herzl, the first street to your right will lead you to Har Hazikaron, and **Yad V'shem**, which means, literally, "a monument and a name." The phrase was taken from Isaiah, "I will give in my house and within my walls a monument and a name better than sons and daughters; I will give them an everlasting name which shall not be cut off." At the end of the street near the Administration Building, there is a long broad path called the **Avenue of the Righteous Gentiles.** Each tree planted along the avenue is named for a non-Jew who endangered his own life to save Jews. Before this honor can be bestowed, a strict judicial procedure is undertaken to establish the validity of the claim. Witnesses are called and the circumstances under which the rescue took place must be authenticated and documented.

The memorial itself lies at the end of the avenue. A cavernous room, always in semi-darkness, houses the Eternal Light that casts a shadow among the stones inscribed with the names of each of the concentration camps in which Jews died. The nearby museum exhibits documents, photographs and implements describing the life and death of these Jews, as well as art work and literature produced by concentration-camp inmates.

A visit to the **Second Temple Model** located on the grounds of the Holyland Hotel is also recommended. Bus No. 12 will take you to the site.

TIME ON YOUR HANDS...

Use your free afternoons and evenings to see where Israelis go and what they do for recreation. The list of places and activities described below is not meant to be exhaustive — only selective.

During the summer (May through October) when you don't want to do anything more energetic than loll about, arrange a picnic or a swimming trip.

Just for Picnics

Sachar Park, in the heart of the City, resembles as closely as possible a lawned, American park. The large, open spaces are fine for an impromptu ball game but you will have to bring everything you need in the way of food and drink for here there are none of the numerous kiosks of other parts of the City. The No. 9 bus passes nearby. Don't be content with settling down at the park's outer periphery, but keep walking till you reach the center, the area used by the surrounding community for fun and games.

If you feel more ambitious, take the bus (the one to Tel Aviv) at the Central Egged Station and travel outside the city limits to **Aqua Bella**, one of Jerusalemite's favorite picnic grounds, and combine your lazy afternoon with a visit to the Crusader Monastery, the waterfalls and the natural springs for which the area is famous. From Aqua Bella, you might walk over to **Abu Ghosh**, a prosperous Arab village with its own share of antiquities.

There is also the **Biblical Zoo**. Compared to American zoos, it's a modest place. But each animal in it has been mentioned in the Bible and chapter and verse are quoted on the animal's cage. The No. 15 bus will drop you off close to the entrance. There is a stand for ice cream and drinks and a few shady corners to eat your sandwiches.

Picnic at a Pool

Jerusalem has no natural waters suitable for swimming and you will have to settle for a man-made waterhole. Some of the pools are really excellent. Don't go to the hotel swimming pools, even though they might be convenient. They are expensive, mostly populated by tourists, usually overcrowded, and you will be heavily charged at the refreshment counters. Instead, try one or a number of the pools where Israeli families wile away the summer days. Mother and the kids go there in the morning, the teenagers arrive at more reasonable hours and the wage-earner comes out to join them right after work.

Brekhat Yerushalayim, the municipal pool, is in the German Colony and can be reached by the No. 4 or 13 bus. Close enough to East Jerusalem for Arab youngsters to get there easily, Brekhat Yerushalayim is the city's "integrated" pool.

Another municipal pool is in **Kiryat Hayovel**, not as centrally located as Brekhat Yerushalayim, but quite pleasant. Take the No. 18 bus to the nieghborhood by the same name.

Kfar Hanofesh in **Ya'ar Yerushalayim** (the Jerusalem Forest) has an excellent swimming pool, but during the summer months it is used almost exclusively by visitors in the nearby youth hostel. It is the only pool in the City which provides facilities for the religious community; men and women use it on different days. Any bus to Har Herzl will do, but there is a goodly walk on the Street of Remembrance till you get to the pool.

There are three excellent swimming pools outside the city limits.

Ma'ale Hakhamishah has the largest pool, umbrellas to protect you from the sun, well-kept lawns, and a refreshment stand. Be sure to buy a package of the kibbutz-grown peaches if you are there at the right time of the year.

Shoresh, the farthest from Jerusalem but a short trip by bus, is at the top of a hill and you can sun and look out at the breathtaking scenery at the same time.

Bet Zayit has three pools; for the toddler, the non-swimmer and the swimmer.

Buses to all swimming pools in the Jerusalem Corridor leave from the Central Bus Station.

Girls and boys with long hair must have bathing caps — a rule in all civilized swimming pools — and everyone should be equipped with the national beach game: two heavy wooden paddles and a small ball, a game that's fine for the faltering amateur and a real workout for the experienced player. They can be purchased at any toy store. Buy the cheapest one available; it's quite as good as the more expensive variety. (By the way, this game is a perfect gift to bring back for sisters, brothers and friends — even for a parent!)

Other Daytime Activities

The **soccer games** on Saturday afternoon are a national institution and even if you don't know the rules too well, it's worthwhile going, at least once, just to see the spectators. The games take place either at the Y.M.C.A. playing field on King David Street or in the soccer field in Katamon. You are lucky if you have a relative or friend living close to the Y.M.C.A. who will invite you to view the game from his porch after Saturday lunch. Every porch in the area is jammed during a Saturday afternoon game. On the day of a game, swarms of people begin arriving in the early afternoon from every direction, and the shouts of the contending fans have been known to awaken the more staid citizens taking their Sabbath afternoon nap as far away as Talbieh.

When you would rather be a participant than a spectator, take a walk with the **Society for the Preservation of Nature.** Though its name is awesome, the society is really an outgoing group and every Saturday afternoon they take anybody and everybody out for a walk in Jerusalem, each week to another place. Their guides are superb (Hebrew only) and they concentrate heavily on the local plant life as well as on archaeology. Find out about the coming walks by watching the billboards. Sometimes as many as 500 strangers will gather to walk together through Jerusalem. This is a must-not-miss activity.

If your Hebrew is weak, however, take the **Municipal Saturday Morning Walks,** which leave at 10 from 34 Jaffa Road.

A conducted **tour of synagogues** leaves every Friday afternoon from the International Cultural Center for Youth, 12A Emek Refa'im Street (Bus No. 4 or 13). Since the meeting time is subject to change, check first at the Government Tourist Information Office at 24 King George Street.

You might also be interested in venturing into the **Valley of the Cross** on a Saturday afternoon. Amble along its paths to the **Youth**

House, the central meeting place of the Scout movement in Jerusalem. You will see many groups engaged in scores of different activities: climbing the sheer cliffs on a rope ladder, learning how to swing on ropes Tarzan style, dancing on the open plaza (particularly nice to see at twilight time), playing basketball or soccer, learning to set up field camps, and generally, having a good time. Be brave and ask if you can join one of the groups that appeals to you. If you have picked the right group, they will be pleased to have a foreigner around to whom they can show off.

As long as you are in the valley, be sure to walk around the **Monastery of the Cross,** the massive, domed building in the lower part of the valley. It was built by the Crusaders in the eleventh century and is still in use today. The rocks and stones everywhere in this valley are themselves quite beautiful and although their location is haphazard it appears as though their placement was carefull planned. In the springtime wild flowers grow between the rocks. Particularly lovely are the delicate cyclamen and the bright red anemone. The cross of Jesus, it is said, was made from an olive tree growing in this valley.

Nighttime Activities

Jerusalem social life still centers largely around the home but more and more nighttime activities are becoming available. Here are some things you might find enjoyable.

A **Saturday night movie** in town is a must. Features change every week on Friday, and the Friday morning papers will give you information on new bills being offered. You may buy your ticket on Friday to be sure to get a seat, as "everyone" goes to the movies on Saturday night, or you can try your luck at the box office immediately after sundown on Saturday. Each movie house has a seating plan which you will find on a wall close to the ticket-seller. Be sure to select the section you want before you get to the point of buying a seat; ticket-sellers are usually an impatient lot. Since most of the movie houses are clustered between Shamai and Hillel Streets, the crush tends to be a little terrifying at first. Fair warning: the seats are hard, the surroundings dilapidated. Even if the film turns out to be less than expected you will enjoy the milling throngs and the feature advertisements, which are often quite clever.

You should go to the **Jerusalem Theater** at least once before you leave the country. The **Jerusalem Symphony Orchestra** and the **Israel**

Chamber Ensemble hold frequent performances there. The latter is particularly fine. Or see a revival of a classic or a translation of a familiar American play if your Hebrew is weak. Only if your Hebrew is pretty good should you attempt a modern Israeli play. If your Hebrew is nonexistent, there may be an English play at **The Khan on** Bethlehem Road near the Railroad Station or a musical being offered elsewhere, or a performance by the **Israel Philharmonic Orchestra** at **Binyenai Ha'ooma.** The Friday Jerusalem Post magazine section gives a complete listing for the week. Tickets may be purchased in advance at the **Cahana Ticket Office, Herbert Samuel Street,** just off Zion Square.

The **Targ Music Center** at **Ein Kerem** features concerts with few performers but high standards. (A lovely half-day jaunt before the concert could consist of a stroll through this suburban village's art galleries and famous old churches and dinner at one of its inns.)

In addition, there are tea houses, restaurants, discotheques, bars, nightclubs and popular entertainment to ease the minds and pocket books of the weary traveller. These, plus special activities for tourists are listed in hotel lobbies and at the Municipal Information Office.

Before leaving Jerusalem, start making plans for your next visit here!

LIST OF ILLUSTRATIONS

FOR YOUR OWN
FOOTNOTES...